Prophecy's Architecture

Prophecy's Architecture

How to Build an End-Times Doctrine

By Cameron Fultz

Strong Tower Publishing
Bellefonte, PA

Strong Tower Publishing

P. O. Box 973

Milesburg, PA 16853

www.strongtowerpublishing.com

ISBN 0-9704330-6-9

Library of Congress Control Number 2005926627

Cover design by Wade Thompson

Table of Contents

Acknowledgements

First of all, I'd like to dedicate this book to my Lord and Savior Jesus Christ, who revealed Himself to me in deeper ways as I internalized entire books of the Bible by reading and listening to them over and over again and by grappling with what they said rather than what I thought they should mean.

I'd like to thank my wife, Teresa, and our five children, Erica, Katrina, Andrea, Noah, and Olivia, for enduring my passion that often saw me cooped up behind a computer or with my nose buried in a stack of Bibles. As they remember my time spent in confinement, I hope they take consolation in also remembering the times I ran down the stairs to excitedly share with them the wonderful things God was teaching me that day.

Foreword

Why do we need another book on prophecy?[1] Some of you may have heard the various prophetic interpretations that seem to be at odds with each other; others may find this diversity of opinion to be new. Books abound that critique others' positions and hail their own understanding. To my knowledge, however, no one has thought to address the question of End-Times prophecy by asking a more foundational question: How does one determine a doctrine in the first place?[2]

By taking the "high road," we appeal to the Christian basics such as how we interpret the Bible, how we recognize that a scripture is specific to the topic we are seeking to understand, and how we let the Scriptures speak for themselves. It is this simple approach that has the ability to suppress human tendencies towards bias, and with any hope, restrain the pride of "knowing the truth" that has virtually stymied healthy dialogue between otherwise loving Christian brothers.

In this book, we will see that the framework of a doctrine is erected much like the structural framework of a building. Once the framework is built, the sub-components fit naturally within, contributing to the whole building. Until now, many people have been trying to build their doctrines of the End Times without following the plan or the example of the Chief Architect. From His perspective, the Architect must see a construction site in vast

---

[1] Why read this book? Because you *can* know the truth. You don't need to be a super-Christian or a "brainiac." God wants you to know the truth. He hasn't hidden the answer.

[2] A doctrine expresses a system of belief. In relationship to God's Word, we determine a doctrine by applying the accepted rules of interpreting the Scriptures and by following the examples or commandments given to us.

confusion, with one set of workers building a lean-to at one corner of the site and another set of workers patting each other on the back for piling together a shanty on the other.

In reality, God has given us all these building components in His Word, His *coherent* Word. It's up to us to faithfully put them together by following the pattern He has established for us and by using the logic with which He has designed us. One wonders why so many Christians are bent on building their own structures, or the structures proclaimed by others, when all they need to do is take the time to read the plans for themselves.

It is too easy to let other people tell you what the Scriptures say. You know where that road leads—to confusion. Why not invest in eternity and really study some of these passages for yourself instead? It is my hope that the principles laid out in this book regarding Bible study basics will not only provide clarity to the confused, but extend into other areas of the Christian life, and that common sense and the simple logic of the Word of God will once again fill our sails.

Cameron Fultz
February, 2004

Part I

Cutting Through the Chaos

1

Can We Really Know
The End-Times Sequence?

Despite what others say, you *can* understand what God's Word says about prophecy. God is the common denominator that holds it all together. God is the author of the Bible. When different parts of God's Word speak specifically about End-Times sequences and events, they all agree. But it is another thing with His redeemed children.

If there is one thing that Christians have disagreed on, it is interpretation as it relates to the prophetic future. Some cults have even arisen because of their leaders' specific interpretations. No wonder some Christians have given up hope of ever understanding prophecy this side of eternity. Bible teachers have even extolled the virtues of being "pan-trib," meaning that "it will all pan out in the end." For those of you who have sat in the pews and rolled your eyes at endless, confusing charts and disconnected verses that don't seem to belong, this book is for you.

I, too, have sat in prophecy classes that expounded upon the many disparate ideas and sensational information about the End Times and the Tribulation. I have been at least one or more times a pre-tribber, post-tribber, amillennialist, pre-wrather, and the like. I have read the books, studied the charts, calculated the prophetic dates, hunted the Antichrist, and wondered if the Mark of the Beast was on the back of the box of my cereal that I ate that morning. There seemed to be no end to the flight of fancy in prophetic interpretation.

The more I learned, however, the more I realized how little I actually understood the pertinent Bible texts. The more I studied and listened to prophecy teachers' tapes, the less time I spent combing through God's Word and seeking to discover the meanings on my own. Finally, the obvious hit me like a train—look to the Bible as the sole source of teaching on the End Times. This book is a record of my journey that traces my steps once I gave up searching for the answers in all the wrong places.

Rather than force-feed you my understanding, I firmly believe that you should strive to understand the solution to the End-Times order and sequence by going through the exercises yourself. We will discuss how one determines a biblical doctrine and what method to use for interpreting the Bible. Once we've laid out the pieces of this critical foundation, we will begin our Bible study. Rather than having you refer to the lesson of one teacher or another, or leaning on your previous understanding, the goal is to have you look to the meaning of scripture fresh and in context.[3] I would rather allow you to look over my shoulders rather than stand on them as if I were some great biblical scholar. I'm no better or more special than you or anyone else in God's eyes. God's Word should be the foundation of all our understanding. We are all in this together, and it is our duty and privilege to search the Scriptures together.

Most of the scriptures quoted in this book use the King James Version (KJV), not because I think it is more special or "authorized" than any other modern translation, but because I still believe it is the most widely accepted translation. If there are significant understandings that can be derived from quoting other English translations, such as the New American Standard Bible (NASB), Amplified, or Greek, I will do so at the relevant points in the text. Suffice it to say that I memorized most of the scripture I know using the KJV, and yet I read mostly out of the Amplified, English Standard Version (ESV), and NASB today.

The goal of any study should ultimately be to glorify Christ. Little did I know just how central that theme was to prophecy until I focused on what God's Word had to say. For the first time, I actually read the real title of a book in the Bible that has probably been more mislabeled than any other. Some people call it

---

[3] To look at scriptures "fresh and in context" should be our goal any time we read the Bible, lest we allow the pride of knowledge to cloud our minds.

"Revelations" and others the "Apocalypse of St. John"; few actually get it right. Do you know its actual title? If not, maybe you should try reading the first verse.

2

A Step-by-Step Process

There are days when I come home and see that something significant has occurred. It's written all over the face of my wife. It's written on the faces of my kids. It's even written on the face of my dog! The silence is awkward as my wife pulls me aside to tell me of the day's events.

"Well, Honey," she says. "I have to tell you about something that happened today...."

Suspense grips me as I wait to hear what it was.

Usually, I have to hear the whole story before I finally learn what happened. It's the waiting that gets me because I have to endure the telling of how the events unfolded. But as difficult as the waiting is, the lengthy story is necessary so that I can properly grasp the context. Every time I try to wrestle out the conclusion before hearing the full story, I tend to make a wrong judgment.

God tells us in His Word that something significant will occur in the future. We must take the time to listen to Him. Our problem is that we, as human beings, want to skip over the long, tedious process and get right to the condensed version from someone who says they know the story. We tend to prefer glossy graphs from a human author over the long hours of searching the texts written by the true Author. In short, we tend to rely on men's word rather than God's Word.

I could just come out and tell you right now that "I found that the Bible teaches a [fill in the blank] understanding of the End Times."[4] But that really means nothing. I would just be another

---

[4] The study of End-Times prophecy is called *eschatology*.

16

man among many who says he knows what God's Word teaches about the subject. You might be persuaded to believe me because I write eloquently, tell entertaining stories, or appeal to your interests. But you would have no way of really knowing what I say is true unless you were to do the research yourself. Because there are so many different views offered today, by so many men who claim to be reading the same Word, we have to be wary of men's views, including mine. The only *real* source is God's Word (Isa. 40:8), not movies, videos, audiotapes, or novels.

Therefore, how does a fallible man like myself write a book on the End Times without succumbing to the trap of "man's opinion interprets God's opinion"? The answer is in the story of what God did in my life as I described in the previous chapter. I had to put away all other sources and teachers, and search only the Bible for my answers. This book tells of that journey, centering on the complete scriptures dealing directly with the End Times and their sequences. Rather than writing a book about how I understand the End Times, I am writing a book that starts at square one—having you, the reader, open your Bible and read it like I did. Yes, just start reading it, take notes, and look for any verses that might have something to do with this topic.

Originally, I had hoped to include chapters and even entire books of the Bible for you to interpret yourself. This way, you could follow my interpretations through these passages and make up your own mind. But in subsequent revisions, I found that readers had an easier time using their own Bibles for study. My hope was (and still is) that, at the end of this study, you will be able to quote scripture rather than a teacher to explain what you believe. And more than this, that you will understand the scriptures you quote in their native context rather than in the context of a teacher's persuasive argument.

You will only know for sure what you know if it comes from the Source of Knowledge. Don't believe me—believe the Word. You will need to read the Bible to find the Bible passages. This is listening to the whole story before you get to the end. *You must know in your own heart that the passages we are studying are indeed the ones we should be studying and that none have been left out.* You need to see for yourself that God has given us a clear and specific teaching on End-Times sequences.

Finding the Chosen Few

"Only five percent of you will ever go on to become architects."

The professor stared into the large audience of students who had now become completely silent.

"Not all of you will have what it takes."

I could hear feet shuffling around the 1920s-era auditorium; I guess I had squirmed, too, knowing that this nine-credit class was required to apply to the College of Architecture and Urban Planning.

"A number of you will get accepted into the architecture program here at the University of Washington, but some of you will not graduate from it. Others may graduate, but will never complete the internship to be eligible to take the state licensing exam. Of those who do take the exam, some will not be able to pass the 12-hour design problem. And even those who eventually become licensed will often gravitate into other fields."

It was true. Of all the people in my graduating class, I know of very few who subsequently went on to become successful architects. The process of determining an End-Times doctrine follows a similar pattern. *The Bible may have many scriptures that mention future events, but there are few that really deal specifically with the subject.* Like all those students who dream about one day becoming architects, only a few of whom will actually go on to do so, only those believers who use the proper approach to studying Scripture will discover what God has to say on the subject. It is this approach to looking for answers from God's Word that we will discuss in this book.

The process is quite simple. When we want to understand what the Bible has to say regarding a particular topic, we search for two things:

- Scriptures that deal *directly* with the subject.
- Scriptures that deal with the subject in any way, even remotely.

Not every scripture will bring the same level of clarity to the issue. In fact, some may be quite general or indirect in their reference to End-Times events. In understanding any biblical doctrine, one must look at all of supporting passages to find the "stand-outs." Some scriptures are very *explicit* (clear and detailed), while others are more *implicit* (general and suggestive). Some deal directly with the topic, while others mention the subject only in passing or in support of another concept. Clearly then, there are some passages to which we should assign more importance than others. Those of greater clarity we could call *primary* and the others *secondary*. Primary passages are what you need to study to develop the framework of a doctrine.

Primary passages represent the plain and core teaching of a doctrine. In this sense, Bible passages are like parts of a building. The primary passages are like columns and beams that carry most of the weight to the foundation. They all work together to hold up the building. If one has built things correctly, this framework should not change as the secondary components are applied.

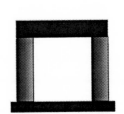

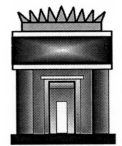

Columns and beams define the shape

The finished shape based on the columns and beams

We can take these lessons into our study of scripture. In the same way that a builder would not place a flimsy 2x4 stud under a beam to carry the entire weight of the building, one would not take an implicit, secondary passage from scripture and use it to support an entire doctrine. This is a very important principle that will keep you from "staking it all" on a passage that was never intended to be the "end all" of a doctrine.

In architecture and construction, remembering this principle can save your life and the lives of others. In fact, there are many rules in place to prevent such blunders. These rules include building codes and the principles of structural engineering. In scripture, we have these rules, as well. They are called the rules of biblical interpretation. These rules will help to keep you from making fundamental errors in interpretation that, ultimately, result in wrong doctrine.

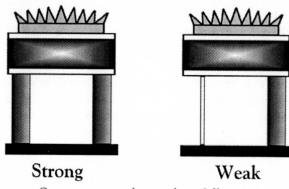

Strong   **Weak**

Common sense does make a difference!

The Bible is not a book filled with mystical ideas and hidden knowledge. Quite the contrary, it is God's eternal Word meant for us to understand and live by. We *can* digest its meaning!

> But He answered and said, "It is written, 'Man shall not live on bread alone, but on every word that proceeds out of the mouth of God....'" (Matt. 4:4, NASB)

In reading the Bible, there are rules that need to be applied. These rules are commonly referred to as the "rules of biblical interpretation." If followed rigorously, they will help the reader understand what God is saying rather than what their imagination is saying. This is likewise true for the builder who follows building codes and blueprints so as not to construct a flimsy structure that is a hazard to safety.

In Chapter 4, we will look at the commonly accepted rules of interpretation. Here, I will tell you this—they follow common sense.

3

Where and How to Start

At our house, we receive two different Christian television channels over the air. One day, I was flipping through the channels and came across a preacher, somewhat stalwart in his composure, but nevertheless sure in every word... and it was God's Word, he boldly asserted. According to him, we were living in the period of the "seventh trumpet" and this was a "sure word of prophecy." As I flipped to the next channel, another preacher had his ire up a notch or two as he declared that we had not yet entered the final seven-year period of God's judgment that would begin with the seven seals, followed by the seven trumpets, then the seven bowls. He seemed to hint that anybody who disagreed with him was teaching false doctrine. Both of them, as certain as they were, could not be right.

How could so many End-Times teachers be so sure, and yet be so wrong? It is the premise of this book that most perspectives on the End Times are the result of reading a book on the subject rather than learning directly from the source—the Book of books, God's Word. It is likely that your pastor was taught a view of eschatology at seminary or picked it up from an interesting book with a catchy title written by an author he respects. Does anyone really have the time to do an exhaustive study of every related passage in the Bible? Given the divergent views on the subject, I question the veracity of any biblical study apart from the Bible as the primary source.

Lay aside the sensational books and novels and drink only from the Words of Life (Phil. 2:16). The order and sequence of the

End Times can be understood if we are willing to humbly set aside our preconceived ideas and apply the rules to let God's Word speak for itself. There are no mysteries involved. These rules are very similar to the ones we use to read any book. If you are serious about understanding God's Word, then I commend you. I am your servant in this journey of discovery. After all, it is our goal to discover what God has put there for us to find.

It is a grievous sin for any of us to perpetuate—no, actually "peddle"—a doctrine of the End Times without thoroughly searching God's Word to get the answer. It is sad to say that we have let pride, the backdoor sin of most Christians, blossom into many doctrines of misinformation. Where some quickly follow the teachings of men, others have simply thrown in the towel. I once condemned people who said they were "pan-trib," but then I realized that these people had simply come to recognize the inconsistencies in the teachings, interpretations, and practices of Christian virtues such as "love thy neighbor"; and disagreements on the End Times can surely shake up the little remaining dross between Christian brothers.

When studying the End Times, then, perhaps the place to begin is in a spirit of repentance. We repent from leaving the understanding of the End Times to others or to those "more knowledgeable" than we are. We repent from defending our own positions and the pride that goes with trying to win arguments rather than being teachable and humble enough to accept a new word from God. We repent from not being like the Bereans, who checked to see if what Paul taught was actually in the Bible. We repent from ignoring or avoiding portions of God's Word. We repent from being too lazy to get to know God's Word. We repent from ignoring the issues and being "pan-trib." We repent from holding onto our reputations rather than to the truth.

I had once considered calling this the "think-less" approach to the End Times. The "think-less" approach simply acknowledges that we all have difficulty separating our biases from our understanding and prefer to support our own opinions rather than being found wrong. If we can develop a method of reading God's Word that minimizes our human influence in the process, we will hear more from God and less from our own imaginations. There is such as process.

Connecting the Dots

As a child, do you remember connecting the numbered dots on a sheet of paper to produce a picture? The picture was always there; we only needed to drag our crayons from point to point to discover what it was. Some kids thought they knew what the picture was before they actually completed the task. As a result, they rushed through to the end, sometimes missing a few points and ending up with a picture different from the one intended. The answer to the End Times is like one of these "connect the dots" exercises. The picture is already there in the Bible, but many have connected the dots too hastily.

To get God's version, we need to stay the course and connect all the dots *in their proper order*. Our order may differ from God's order if we are too hasty or too biased. God's Word is perfectly clear about the End Times when this approach is used. I don't mean literally drawing lines in your Bible, but doing something more conceptual. The dots are simply "common denominators," such as phrases, events, and sequences that link two or more passages of scripture. When we find a common event or sequence between two passages, we don't ignore it or re-interpret it according to our bias. We draw a line between them, stand back, and acknowledge that a connection exists, whether it agrees with our understanding or not. In fact, the less we think we know what the Bible teaches on the matter, the greater our capacity to learn the truth. Why? Because we allow God's Word to communicate to us. We depend upon Him for the answer.

Allow me to restate this. During this process, many of you may have been taught a certain perspective on the End Times that will be challenged. I will not challenge it; rather, this method and what the Bible text actually says will challenge it. We may find scripture verses to connect that your accepted view will not tolerate. The problem we have today is that many teachers expound many different views, each claiming to be right and biblically sound. We have to tackle this subject at a more basic level, one that avoids bias as much as possible.

If God's Word is coherent, then the place to begin is with the most specific, clear, and detailed passages on the sequence of the End Times. Figuring out which passages to use is no mystery. It actually involves as little thought and, therefore, as little bias as possible: the process is called *discovery*. To employ the process of discovery, search through the entire Bible to find any passage that you think might deal with the End Times. *Coldly and callously* create three columns on a sheet of paper, graduating them from the most clear to the most ambiguous, and place each scripture in one of these columns. There will always be a natural division of three, with an extreme on either side and a middle ground between them. Where is the bias in that?

Once you have isolated the most clear and detailed passages, begin to compare them to one to another by looking for common denominators. Only compare the clearest passages. Never develop a doctrine using an ambiguous scripture. Herein lies the trap of many wayward End-Times views. When one is trying to protect their own perspective or reputation, obscure passages tend to get elevated to hubris-like prominence. There is no blame to be cast here. It's the natural, human thing to do. Certain verses that are not even specific to the topic of the End Times, but mention aspects of it in support of another point, are often used as core verses in certain End-Times doctrines. That is like trying to fix an airplane engine with spare parts from a bicycle shop. Just as there are better places to buy airplane components, so there are better scriptures that address End-Times sequences. To understand God's Word on the topic, we must stick to the passages that explicitly relate to the End Times and that provide clear and detailed information. Straying from this approach allows entry of your own bias by capitalizing on a phrase or idiom that proves what you already want to believe.

Passages dealing with End-Times prophecy are strewn throughout the Bible. I whole-heartedly encourage you to embark on this journey into God's Word. It may take awhile, but the fruit of your study will abide forever.

As an aid, I have developed a list of every Bible passage I have found dealing with the topic of the End Times. If I had just stopped there, I probably would have joined the ranks of other "pan-tribbers." But as I discovered, the heart of the issue revolves around the order and sequence of events. That became my criteria—to search out and *find the most detailed scriptures that clearly lay out order and sequence as their primary subject.* Of course, not everybody is willing to take the time to do this. It is much easier to "proclaim" a truth than to *find* the truth. But God's Word is worth it, isn't it?

To the best of my knowledge, I have not overlooked any scripture dealing with the End Times. I provide my list for you in Chapter 5 so that you may compare it with your own. I have found only six passages explicit enough to form the real basis of a doctrine. They are analogous to the skeletal structure of a building, because the foundation, beams, and columns hold everything in place. In actuality, it didn't take that long to find these particular passages. Most of us are already familiar with them. The longer process involved studying the rest of scripture to determine whether I had missed any passages or whether some were more relevant than others.

Of the hundreds of general End-Times passages, there arose a group of about 20 that were "in between." These passages are not as explicit as the top group, but not as general as the greater group. Just as windows shed more light and doorways provide access points, this middle group helps to better define certain End-Times issues. They should not, however, be used to define a doctrine any more than doors should be used to hold up a large structure (the last time I checked, doors were not rated as load-bearing columns).

Moving from the middle group into the vast remainder, these passages represent the finishing details that round out the whole counsel of God. A structure they do not make, but taken together, they add depth and overall beauty.

Our interpretation will be defined by the clearest passages, then elaborated and embellished upon by the others. The primary components establish the bounds and general sequence, while the secondary components increase our understanding of what God has already defined. As I mentioned, the only assumption that I made was that God is coherent. If God is coherent, then His Word is coherent. If His Word is coherent, then we should be able to find parallels and alignments between the most clear and detailed passages dealing directly with the subject we are researching. In this sense, God is the Prophetic Common Denominator. He is the source of all these teachings. If there is confusion, it lies in our biased interpretation or laziness in studying God's Word, not in the Word itself.

In the next chapter, we will establish how the Bible is to be interpreted.[5] Following that, we will introduce all of the prophetic passages that deal with the future we call the Last Days, the Tribulation, or the End Times. This includes the Second Coming, the Rapture, the Millennium, the Day of the Lord, Armageddon, and similar topics. These scriptures will be laid out in the three groupings that I have described. I encourage you to read as many of these passages as possible. In Part Two, we will examine how they inter-link.

Some will say that scholars have debated the meaning of End-Times prophecies for centuries. By saying this, they are implying that no one can really know the answer. But that is no excuse for not looking into these matters yourself. By talking about the debate, rather than the Word, we are falsely elevating the teachings of men. Given so many opinions on this topic, we should be seeking out study methods that remove as much of the bias as possible. Wouldn't it be ironic if such a method led us to a sound understanding?

---

[5] The study of how one interprets the Bible is called *hermeneutics*.

4

Rules of Interpretation

When you read any book, you interpret its meaning. A novel makes sense because you follow the rules you learned in school. You know how a figure of speech works and how to recognize the difference between literal and symbolic language. These common-sense rules apply to reading the Bible, too.

God is your Creator and the inventor of communication, understanding, and reason. He designed you to see, hear, read, and comprehend. The Bible is our owner's manual, straight from the factory. The One who knows everything put it together so that the end product can function to its best potential. God wants us to understand. He is not trying to trick us or confuse us.

> Now these things happened to them as an example, but they were written down for our instruction, on whom the end of the ages has come. (1 Cor. 10:1, ESV)

> I will instruct thee and teach thee in the way which thou shalt go: I will guide thee with mine eye. (Psalm 32:8)

> Know therefore and understand.... (Dan. 9:25)

God is not trying to hide the meaning from us. You can trust what God says as true. Opinion is irrelevant. You can choose to believe it or choose not to. Those who choose not to believe it tend to "spiritualize" the text, looking for hidden meanings. Rather than letting God determine the meaning, they determine their own. The problem with that method is that all interpretations are valid and no one is wrong. Clearly, this is not God's intention. The Word of

God is meant to be understood and acted upon accordingly. This is sometimes referred to as the *literal hermeneutic* or the *literal systematic approach* to understanding and interpreting the Bible.

I hold to this "literal" understanding, believing that God has something specific to say to us, and that we can understand it plainly. As such, there are a few rules that should be followed when reading the Bible.

1. The Holy Spirit: The "owner's manual" says that we need to be oiled to function properly. If we are not oiled, our parts will not move easily. The Holy Spirit living inside us is our oil. He makes it so that we can understand. We must rely on God's Spirit to teach us and guide us through the Scriptures.

> But the Comforter (Counselor, Helper, Intercessor, Advocate, Strengthener, Standby), the Holy Spirit, Whom the Father will send in My name [in My place, to represent Me and act on My behalf], He will teach you all things. And He will cause you to recall (will remind you of, bring to your remembrance) everything I have told you. (John 14:26, Amplified)

This is the design. This is how it works. Why? Probably because the Holy Spirit is God and He wrote the Bible, using men who otherwise tend to be self-deceptive.

> But know this first of all, that no prophecy of Scripture is a matter of one's own interpretation, for no prophecy was ever made by an act of human will, but men moved by the Holy Spirit spoke from God. (2 Peter 1:20–21, NASB)

The Creator spoke through His created beings. The Inventor prepared these vehicles to communicate His message. Their personalities and writing styles were predetermined by God to reflect that message. Why did God use men's personalities? God is a person and He invented personalities.[6] He has every right. And He has every privilege to do so. God is the Prophetic Common Denominator. He wrote the Bible and makes it coherent. Even through these personalities, the various passages must make sense. God is a God of order.

---

[6] Actually three Persons in One: Triune.

2. Compare scripture with scripture. The Bible is its own best interpreter. A coherent Bible is the result of a coherent Creator and God of order who wants His words to be understood. When God communicates specifically on the topic of the End-Times sequence, we should expect to find parallels, alignments, and points of connection. This also means that when we run across what we believe to be an apparent contradiction, something to which we have yet to find the answer, this is all the more reason to pray and seek the Holy Spirit's guidance.

3. Learn historical background. The Bible is a historical book. Because we live in a modern age, we may not be familiar with customs and imagery that readers hundreds of years ago took for granted. For instance, when was the last time you read a sealed scroll delivered to you by messenger? Do you know how many seals a scroll had or whether it was common to write on both sides of the scroll? What is the purpose of a seal? As another example, prophetic passages frequently refer to the historical empire and city of Babylon. What was the attitude of the people who lived in Babylon? Do you know where the city was located? Were there any important rivers that flowed through it? How did the city finally fall and who was involved? All of these things pertain to a proper understanding of End-Times imagery. The Bible often points to things that happened in the past as examples of how they will be ultimately fulfilled in the future.

Reference material that sticks to historical facts rather than the interpretation of those facts would serve you well. Some Bible encyclopedias and handbooks accomplish this well.

4. Seek the intended meaning. If the plain sense makes sense, then you understand. Don't look for hidden messages with mystical meanings. The Author will give you clues so that you can understand what is written as either symbolic or literal. The flow of the discussion or story will also provide you with the context. There's nothing worse than taking a verse out of context and using it to prove a point that it was never intended to make.

5. Understand the "less clear" in light of the "more clear." This goes back to our discussion of primary and secondary passages. Let the more specific scriptures interpret the other, less specific scriptures, never the other way around. Some passages will be more specific to the End-Times sequence than others. It is these clear and detailed passages that will make up the core understanding.

There you have it: the basic rules of interpretation. Some scholars use different words, acrostics, or split the categories into more specific divisions. But essentially, there are only a few foundational principles as I have expounded upon them. It really is that simple. The hard part is being consistent in your application.

Next, let's apply these rules together and see what we get.

5

Finding the Clearest Counsel of God

"The Bible is the Book of books without comparison or equal," I said as I hefted my Bible up before the Sunday school class. "You can have full confidence in what the Word of God says. We have seen the manuscript evidences and the latest archaeological evidences that all show us that the Bible we read today is communicating the exact same message as when it was originally penned and distributed thousands of years ago! Remember 40x40=1600! In other words, the Bible was written by over 40 different authors in 40 different walks of life over a 1600-year period, all communicating the same message—in fact, the same theme: God's plan for man's redemption. And these authors wrote about many controversial subjects and yet remained in agreement because it was the Holy Spirit who moved them to write as we see in 2 Peter 1:20–21 and 2 Tim. 3:16. The comparative challenge for today would be to see if we could get even 10 authors, all from the *same* walk of life and time, to agree on even *one* controversial subject!"

And of course, that is the challenge for us today. We do, indeed, see many pastors and Bible teachers all writing on one controversial subject, the End Times, with little agreement. It is not the Word of God that is the issue; it is men and their biases ("...let God be true, but every man a liar..." Romans 3:4). How do we find the truth? By starting from the source of truth.

Sanctify them through thy truth: thy word is truth. (John 17:7)

Do you remember our earlier discussion of coldly and callously creating three columns to sort out the Bible verses to minimize personal bias? In this chapter, we will look at the graduated list I developed of specific, in-between, and ambiguous texts. You will need to verify this list for yourself, particularly the first column of specific passages, because it is with these that we will build our doctrine. There is no point in going on if you do not agree with me on the primary passages.

The clearest and most detailed passages as they relate to the order and sequence of End-Times events are listed for you in Group 1: The Main and Plain. The less explicit passages that still have much to contribute are listed for you in Group 2: The In-Between. The general passages that have End-Times themes but little or no bearing on the timing of End-Times sequences have been collected in Group 3: The Vague and Indistinct.

It is clear that if I were studying the ministry of the Holy Spirit, my list would be different. It would also be different if I were studying a different aspect of the End Times, such as the Antichrist, the Beast Empires, or the Day of the Lord. The following lists of verses relate only to the study of the order and sequence of End-Times events, including the 70th Seven, the Great Tribulation, the Rapture, the Abomination of Desolation, and the beginning of God's wrath.

Now let's take a closer look at the three groups. First, the primary passages: The Main and Plain.

Group 1: The Main and Plain

The Olivet Discourse (Matthew 24, Mark 13)
Daniel 9:24–27
1 Thessalonians 4:13–5:11
2 Thessalonians 2:1–12
Daniel 11:35–36, 12
The Revelation of Jesus Christ

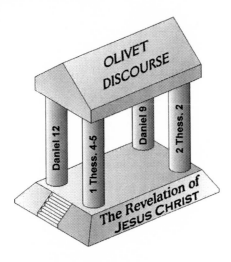

The figure shown above illustrates these six primary passages and how they form a structure.

Now let's look at Group 2:

Group 2: The In-Between		
Psalm 18:1–20	Isaiah 64:1–5	Matthew 13:37–43
Psalm 110	Ezekiel 37–39	Matthew 25
Isaiah 2:10–22	Daniel 2:19–45, 3	Luke 17:22–36
Isaiah 13:9–13	Daniel 7	Luke 21:5–38
Isaiah 24	Daniel 8	Romans 11:25–26
Isaiah 26:19–27:1	Joel	1 Corinthians 15:20–56
Isaiah 28:15–22	Zechariah 12-14	2 Peter 2:4–9, 3:3–13

Now let's look at Group 3: The Vague and Indistinct:[7]

---

[7] Determining whether a passage of scripture is prophetic is not an exact science. Some passages referring to Christ's First Coming were not so easily recognized until after the event. I am sure the more I delve into God's Word, the longer my Group 3 list of prophetic verses will become.

Group 3: The Vague and Indistinct

Genesis 3:15
Genesis 7:1–16
Genesis 18:18–19
Genesis 22:18
Genesis 26:4
Leviticus 16:30-34
Leviticus 25:8–55
Leviticus 26
Deuteronomy 18:20–22
Deuteronomy 28:64–66
Deuteronomy 30
Deuteronomy 31:16–18
2 Samuel 7:12–19
Psalm 2
Psalm 69:28
Psalm 72
Psalm 79
Psalm 96:9–13
Psalm 97
Psalm 118:19–22
Isaiah 1:21–28
Isaiah 2
Isaiah 3
Isaiah 4
Isaiah 9:7
Isaiah 10:20–23
Isaiah 11:4–10
Isaiah 14:3-23
Isaiah 19:18–25
Isaiah 25
Isaiah 26
Isaiah 27
Isaiah 28:20–22
Isaiah 30:18–28
Isaiah 34:1–10
Isaiah 35
Isaiah 43:1–13
Isaiah 46:13
Isaiah 49:6–16
Isaiah 51:3–11
Isaiah 54:5–17
Isaiah 60
Isaiah 61:2–11
Isaiah 62
Isaiah 63:1–6

Isaiah 64
Isaiah 65:8–25
Isaiah 66:10–24
Jeremiah 30
Jeremiah 31:1–14
Ezekiel 2:8–3:6
Ezekiel 7:19–20
Ezekiel 20:33–40
Ezekiel 34:22–31
Ezekiel 36:24–38
Ezekiel 40
Ezekiel 41
Ezekiel 42
Ezekiel 43
Ezekiel 44
Ezekiel 45
Ezekiel 46
Ezekiel 47
Ezekiel 48
Daniel
Hosea 1:10–11
Hosea 2:14–23, 3:5
Hosea 6:1–3
Hosea 11:8–11
Amos 5:18–20
Micah 2:12–13
Micah 4:1–8
Habakkuk 3:8–13
Zephaniah 1:14–2:3
Zephaniah 3:8–20
Haggai 2:6–9
Haggai 2:21–23
Zechariah
Malachi 3:2–6
Malachi 4:5–6
Matthew 7:21–23
Matthew 8:29
Matthew 10:16–23
Matthew 19:28–30
Matthew 23:39
Matthew 26:29
Luke 12:35–40
Luke 18:6–8
Luke 22:28–30
John 3:18

John 3:36
John 5:24–29
John 12:31
John 14:1–14
John 16:11
John 21:21–25
Acts 1:6–7
Acts 2:14–24
Acts 3:21–26
Acts 17:30–31
Romans 1:18–32
Romans 5:3–5
Romans 8:18–25
Romans 11
Romans 14:11–12
Romans 16:25–27
1 Corinthians 1:7–8
1 Corinthians 3:9–16
1 Corinthians 13:9–10
2 Corinthians 5:10
Galatians 3:6–9
Ephesians 5:27
Ephesians 6:18
Philippians 2:9–10
Colossians 2:17
1 Thessalonians 1:10
1 Thessalonians 2:19
1 Thessalonians 3:3–4
1 Thessalonians 3:13
2 Thessalonians 1:4–10
1 Timothy 4:1–2, 6:14
2 Timothy 3:1–5
2 Timothy 4:3–4, 8
Titus 2:12–13
Hebrews 9:28
Hebrews 10:25
Hebrews 11:9–10, 16
James 5:7–11
1 Peter 1:7
1 Peter 4:12–19
1 John 2:18
1 John 2:28
1 John 4:3
2 John 1:7
Jude 6–7

It is easy to muddy the waters by holding onto the pride of knowledge. Review the six primary passages from Group 1 and compare them with others that you may think are just as good. Better yet, read the entire Bible, searching for passages on End-Times sequences and go through the exercise yourself.

Remember that the primary source texts must show the following three characteristics better than any other passages in the Bible. They must:

1. Be on the topic of the End Times.
2. Discuss End-Times order and sequence.
3. Be specific, clear, and detailed.

Following is a brief description of the six primary passages I have listed in The Main and Plain and an explanation for why I chose them as primary passages:

Daniel 9:24–27: Rather than starting with a bias such as, "This scripture is about the Messiah and was fulfilled at the cross," or getting into debates about gaps, I'm looking for passages that could be plainly understood as End-Times scriptures with sequential detail. In this case, I chose Dan. 9:24–27 as a primary passage because it provides specific numbers and order and can be understood at face value as referring to the End Times.

There are three reasons this passage fits this criteria:

First, this passage talks about when God is going to fulfill His promises to Israel. It is a prophecy given in response to the fervent prayer of Daniel, pleading for the nation while they were still captives in faraway Babylon. As far as I know, God has not literally fulfilled any of the promises to Israel listed in verse 24. As a whole, they are promises from God to Daniel that the wayward heart and stiff neck of the Israelites will one day be gone. If we remain consistent with the grammar, this promise still awaits a literal fulfillment. Just as the city was literally rebuilt and the Messiah was literally cut off, so must the other aspects of this prophecy be literally fulfilled.

Second, the passage begins with the declaration that "70 weeks" are determined or decreed as a timeline until the things in verse 24 are to be accomplished. Some translations use the term "70 sevens" or "70 sets of seven" for further clarification so that we understand them as years rather than weeks. Daniel understood them as years, for he knew that one of the predictions in this timeline was the reconstruction of Jerusalem, a process that takes decades rather than weeks.

Critical in understanding this timeline of "70 sets of seven" is how it is broken up into three distinct segments. The first segment calls for seven sets of seven, or 49 years, for the city to be built in troubled times—which is exactly what happened, as recorded in Ezra and Nehemiah. The second set of seven adds another 62 sets of seven, or 434 more years until the Anointed One, the Messiah (or "Christ" in the Greek), was to be cut off from the land of the living. The last set of seven is that seven-year period many people refer to as the "Tribulation" or "70th Seven," which plays a major role in many End-Times views.

Thirdly, the terminology employed refers to the "end," with "desolations," "abominations" leading to a "consummation," with judgments being "poured out." All this is related to the timeline and the ultimate fulfillment for Israel (Daniel's holy people and holy city, Jerusalem, in verse 24).

Taken together, these provide a clear and detailed outline of sequences related to the End Times.

Daniel 11:35–36, 12:1–13: This passage is part of a larger vision beginning in Daniel 10. The passage begins to take on an End-Times twist in Dan. 11:35–36 with the words, "even to the time of the end" and "till the indignation be accomplished...determined shall be done." The phrase "time of the end" is repeated again in Dan. 12:4, 9, and "the end" is repeated in Dan. 12:13. By its own admission, this passage is speaking about the End Times.

There are also some specific time periods assigned to events that originate with the Abomination of Desolation, first described in Dan. 12:11–12. For instance, 1,260 days is half of a set of seven (or half of a "week") as described in Dan. 9:24–27. Therefore, from the midst of the seven, there will be 1,260 days until it is over. Additional events and sequences are given in Dan. 12:1–3, referencing a final time of tribulation for God's people and, ultimately, the resurrection of the just.

The Olivet Discourse (Matthew 24):[8] Again, as we approach the Olivet Discourse, we must put aside our taught biases. The reason the Olivet Discourse is recognized as one of the most clear and detailed passages is because in it, Jesus directly answers two questions from His disciples regarding the end of the world and His return. Jesus provides us with sequences (see verses 8–9, 13–15, 21–22, and 29–30), with many references to the "end." Jesus also wanted to make sure this teaching was clear (see verses 4, 23, 25, and 33).

1 Thessalonians 4:13–5:11: The Rapture (gathering together, catching up)[9] to the Lord happens when Jesus returns. This passage is perhaps the clearest and most detailed of all those that discuss this specific End-Times event. Signs and a specific order accompany the Rapture. I also find no reason to end the discussion at the man-made chapter break, for Chapter 5 continues to add additional sequencing, qualifications, and imagery.

2 Thessalonians 2:1–12: Paul seeks to clarify what he taught in 1 Thessalonians by discussing the return of Christ, the gathering together, and Day of Christ in this second of his two-part series of letters. He outlays a very specific sequence in 2 Thess. 2:3–4, and then goes to great detail, expanding on the teaching to tie it into other known teachings in verses 8–12.

The Book of Revelation: It probably goes without saying why I would include this book of the Bible. It has many End-Times sequences, abundant detail, and is clearly focused on Christ's return and the eternal state. After all, Rev. 1:1 says this book's proper title is "The Revelation of Jesus Christ." Many people get bogged down by the imagery and ignore the clear similarities its contents have with other passages in the Bible.

These are the six passages that alone form the framework of End-Times doctrine, not because of what I say, but because of what they say. Just as I took the time to discover that these six

---

[8] Mark 13 is a retelling of this same sermon, while Luke 21 is not. For an explanation of the differences between these discussions, and how it affects the End-Times sequences, see Appendix C.

[9] The term "Rapture" is not used in the Bible unless you are reading a Latin translation. However, it is still a good term to describe what we translate into English as "caught up" and "gather together."

represent the clearest and most detailed teaching in the Bible on the topic of End-Times sequencing, so must you, the reader, come to your own acknowledgment of this fact. If you already hold to a particular view, I encourage you to pull out your "champion" verses and put them to the test.

Do Others Pass the Test?

Let's look at a two of the most common passages others often cite as key passages on End-Times sequencing and see if they can pass the muster.

1 Corinthians 15:20–56 (specifically 51–52):

Behold, I show you a mystery; We shall not all sleep, but we shall all be changed, in a moment, in the twinkling of an eye, at the last trumpet: for the trumpet shall sound, and the dead shall be raised incorruptible, and we shall be changed. (1 Cor. 15:51–52)

Because of its reference to "the last trump," many people like to use this as one of the primary passages for determining the timing of the Rapture. But I ask you, is this passage on the topic of the End Times? No, it doesn't meet the first qualification. It's on a different topic. Sure, it has a fascinating reference to the Rapture, but this reference is in support of Paul's point about the nature of the resurrected body. And Paul's discussion of the resurrected body is in context of a larger discussion on the resurrection and its power over death. We have to let the primary passages on the topic tell us the timing, and this isn't one of them.

James 5:7–11:

Be patient therefore, brethren, unto the coming of the Lord. Behold, the husbandman waiteth for the previous fruit of the earth, and hath long patience for it, until he receive the early and latter rain. Be ye also patient; stablish your hearts: for the coming of the Lord draweth nigh. Grudge not one against another, brethren, lest ye be condemned: behold, the judge standeth before the door. Take, my brethren, the prophets, who have spoken in the name of the Lord, for an example of suffering affliction, and of patience. Behold, we count them

happy which endure. Ye have heard of the patience of Job,
and have seen the end of the Lord; that the Lord is very
pitiful, and of tender mercy.

Because of its reference to "the coming of the Lord is
near...at the door," this passage is used by many as a proof text
that Jesus will return at any moment. But, I ask you, is this the
goal and topic of this scripture?

The context of this passage goes back to the end of James 4.
The reference to the "Judge at the door" is not meant to be a
doctrinal statement regarding an imminent return of Christ, but
rather is a reference to its previous usage in James 4:11–12,
pointing to the fact that we don't know when we will meet our
Maker and face justice for how we have treated one another. It is
making a point about the brevity of life in the context of Christian
living rather than being a clear End-Times teaching. James is
chiding these Christians for their quarreling and prideful
confidence in thinking that they know what tomorrow holds. The
plans they make and riches they accumulate (James 5:1–6) may be
for nothing. They could die and stand before the true Judge who
will set things aright. This is the point of the passage.

These are just two examples of passages used by those on
opposite ends of the spectrum as to when they believe the Rapture
is to occur. It is not my desire to get into an exhaustive discussion
on the timing of the Rapture at this time. Rather, it is to point out
that these passages and others like them, such as John 14:1–3 or
Titus 2:12–14, are not specific, clear, and detailed teachings on the
timing of any End-Times event or sequence and therefore do not
belong in the foundational formulation of End-Times doctrine.
This is a role reserved solely for the primary passages.

Once you are satisfied that the six passages I have identified
are the clearest and most detailed scriptures on the topic of End-
Times sequences, then we can move on to building the framework
in Part Two.

Part II

Except the LORD build the house, they labour in vain
that build it.

(Psalm 127:1)

Cameron Fultz

6

Reading the Blueprint

For many people, the topic of prophecy is like a cornfield maze. The stalks are so tall that they can't see above them, and the growth so thick that they have no idea which way the path will turn. They might be tempted to think that God is just toying with them. If God really wanted them to understand His Word about the End Times and its sequences, wouldn't He have provided a pattern to show the way? Well, He *has* provided a way. What better teacher is there than our Lord Jesus Christ? What better example than when He was teaching the disciples? What better time than when He was discussing the topic?

Jesus knew that we were helpless without His example. This is why He had to frequently explain things to the disciples. Remember the time Jesus said to watch out for the leaven or yeast of Israel's religious leaders (Matt. 16:5–12)? The disciples all looked around to see if they had brought bread, which has leaven in it. But Jesus was not talking about food. He told them plainly that they were to watch out for the teaching of these hypocrites that spreads like leaven. Likewise, Jesus has given us a key to unlocking the seemingly confusing maze of prophecy.

> When ye therefore shall see the Abomination of Desolation, spoken of by Daniel the prophet, stand in the holy place, (whoso readeth, let him understand). (Matt. 24:15)

In these passages, Jesus is highlighting a common event that is of great significance to the sequence so that we can see the coherence of God's Word and how it all fits together. The key is to

43

look for the common events, alignments, and parallels. Jesus knew that we of little understanding have the tendency to make hasty assumptions. There is even an admonition here from Matthew to the reader so we don't miss it. The Greek word "to understand" literally means "to exercise the mind."[10] It is a challenge to figure out the link and observe the pattern.

In this part of the book, Chapters 7–15, we will "connect the dots" between the clearest and most detailed scriptures that help us understand the architecture of End-Times prophecy. Just as, in the previous section, we coldly and callously made three columns to find the most specific scriptures using minimal bias, here we will coldly and callously look for common events, signs, or parallels and draw connections to see if they hold.

As these connecting lines are drawn, a pattern will appear. We did not make it up. It already existed, placed there by its Author, waiting for us to figure it out and read the blueprint. I believe God did this to humble us. All Christians need humbling, even great Christian leaders. God has made a child-like method to confound the paper-rustling of scholars.

We will start where Jesus set the example, by drawing lines between the Olivet Discourse and the passages in Daniel that discuss the Abomination of Desolation. It should not surprise you that, to help us understand His teaching in the Olivet Discourse, Jesus is sending us to the very two Old Testament passages we discovered to be primary passages. Is it a coincidence that these three passages—the Olivet Discourse (Matthew 24), Daniel 9, and Daniel 12—are primary passages on the topic of End-Times sequencing by their own admission?

---

[10] Strong's G3539. A concordance will reference this number to a definition. G=Greek.

7

The Abomination of Desolation

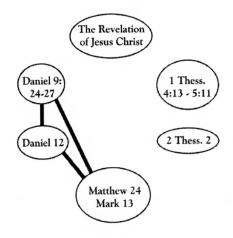

Daniel 9 ⇔ Daniel 12 ⇔ Matthew 24

The first link comes from Jesus. He is our example and our teacher. We are told to connect what He is teaching in Matthew 24 with the events about which Daniel wrote, events that relate to the Abomination of Desolation.

What is the Abomination of Desolation? Simply put, it is an unholy act or thing that prevents the temple in Jerusalem from being used for holy rituals. The deceptions, betrayals, and persecutions described by Jesus against "you" are directly related to this act of desecration of the innermost temple sanctum where the sacrifices were carried out.

What does Jesus have to say about the significance of the abomination?

In Matthew 24, Jesus is answering the disciples' two questions about His Second Coming and the end of the world. As part of the answer, He explains the things that lead up to His return at the end of the present age.[11] Key to the "end of the age" is this "Abomination of Desolation" that affects "you," the disciples.[12]

One of the reasons the "you" refers to disciples of Christ living to see these times, rather than to the nation of Israel only (as many teach, thus making this passage irrelevant to the Church and, therefore, to our discussion of End-Times sequence), is the Great Commission in Matt. 28:19–20. The marching orders given to the Church through the disciples are to pass on Jesus' teachings, which include Matthew 24. Those who prefer to teach otherwise are on dangerous footing. There really is no "plain and simple" way to understand this passage being about Israel and Armageddon, rather than about the Church at the return of Christ in the midst of the 70th Seven.

We have to let the scriptures draw their own conclusions. Let's just understand these passages at their most basic level and see if it all pans out. Let's allow Jesus to make the first connection and then we can follow. In the Olivet Discourse, Jesus directly ties these times of horrible upheaval to the timeline and troubles mentioned in Daniel. Matthew 24 appears to be directed at

---

[11] It is immediately after these "tribulations" that Jesus says He will return (Matt. 24:29–30).

[12] Many people with a preset doctrine prefer that this passage speak about Israel and Armageddon, making the "you" refer generically to all Israel instead of to Christians. Understandably, there is some confusion about this issue. The confusion arises in the interpretation of Matthew 24, Mark 13, and Luke 21. Some see Mark 13 and Luke 21 as parallel passages to Matthew 24, while others see the only parallel to Matthew 24 as Mark 13, with Luke 21 being a preceding public discourse. The resolution to this debate is important because, in Luke 21, Jesus appears to be speaking only to Israel; while both Matthew 24 and Mark 13 are clearly private night-time teachings given only to a select group of the disciples. Jesus did, on various occasions, take private time to further explain to His disciples what He taught publicly. For more on this subject, see Appendix C.

Christians, while Daniel is directed at Israel, but the two are linked together by the Abomination of Desolation.

What does Daniel have to say about the significance of the abomination?

To understand the significance, we need to understand a little bit of Daniel's background and the times of his writings. Daniel lived to see the day that the beloved temple in Jerusalem was destroyed by the Babylonian army in the sixth century B.C. He was one of the first captives of Israel taken to Babylon. Daniel longed for Israel's return to Jerusalem so that the nation's relationship could be restored with God. While in captivity, Daniel came upon the prophetic writings of Jeremiah that predicted 70 years of punishment for Israel because they had forgotten to trust in their God (Jer. 25:11–12, 29:10). He then deeply sought after God for restoration and understanding.

God held Daniel in high esteem (Eze. 14:14, 20), and as such gave him a complete answer to his question. Yes, Israel would return after the 70 years, but they would do so no better than before the punishment. According to Levitical law, Israel would need to be punished seven more times for her sins (Lev. 26:18). Daniel receives this explanation in Dan. 9:24–27, where we learn about the seven times more of 70 years, or the "70 sevens." Daniel is told that these 70 sevens represent the completion of Israel's punishment, and that when those years are over, Israel's relationship will be completely and literally restored. Stop and think about what that means, especially today, thousands of years after Christ.

So that Daniel and future generations will know to take this restoration literally, the sequence is broken into three segments—7, 62, and 1 "sets of seven." Just as the city will be rebuilt after seven sets, so will the Messiah be literally cut off after another 62 sets. And far into the future, during the End Times, a final seven will occur, involving the greatest of all distress and an abomination in the temple. Daniel 9:24–27 and Dan. 11:35–12:13 speak of these times.[13]

---

[13] Daniel 11:31 records another reference to an abomination that occurred during the Maccabean revolt in 168 B.C. Jesus is not referring to this historical event, since He is speaking of an event that has yet to occur in

In Dan. 9:27, the angelic messenger tells Daniel that the abomination will occur at the midpoint of that last set of seven, the 70th Seven (or "Tribulation" in some circles).[14] That leaves 1,260 days until the end of the prophesied 70 sets of seven.[15]

> ...and in the midst of the week he shall...make it desolate.
> (Dan. 9:27)

At the end of that last set of seven, 1,260 days after the midpoint, the most Holy will be anointed.

> Seventy weeks are determined...to anoint the most Holy.
> (Dan. 9:24)

A typical Hebrew would understand the term "most Holy" to mean the Holy of holies in the temple in Jerusalem. Put simply, this means that the sanctuary will be purified at the end of those 70 sevens. A precise number is given, tied to a specific deed. And if the sanctuary is literally anointed, then it means that the abomination is no longer there. The maximum duration of defilement is 1,260 days.

However, in Chapter 12, the angelic messenger says the *effect* of the abomination will linger for an additional 30 days after the last set of seven is complete:

> And from the time...the abomination that maketh desolate set up, there shall be a thousand two hundred and ninety days.
> (Dan. 12:11)

This creates a bit of an enigma for us. How can the abomination last 1,290 days when it is removed after 1,260 days? Does it "run away" from the sanctuary so that the Holy of holies

---

the future. With the phrase "until the time of the end (NKJ)," Dan. 11:35 jumps forward from events that have already transpired to future events that have yet to be fulfilled during the End Times.

[14] See Appendix B for an explanation of why I believe there is a gap between the 69th and 70th Sevens of Dan. 9:24–27.

[15] A prophetic year is made up of 360 days. This is how the Jewish calendar works—twelve 30-day months. A set of seven years is 2,520 days. The midpoint of a set of seven is 1,260 days, or 42 months.

can be anointed on schedule? How can the abomination continue in power even though it has been physically removed? The answer is found back in Dan. 9:27:

> ... abominations he shall make it desolate, even until the consummation, and that determined shall be poured upon the desolate. (Dan. 9:27)

Notice here that "he" is making the Holy of holies desolate. This "he" refers back verse 26, to the prince who is to come, who is described as one who will destroy.[16] Some translations identify "he" with the last word of Dan. 9:27 and render it as "desolator" instead of "desolate" (RSV, NRSV). This passage would then read, "and that determined shall be poured upon the desolator." In other words, this "he" is the personification of the Abomination of Desolation, the one many would call the Antichrist.[17] This is how the Abomination of Desolation lasts another 30 days, because the abomination is really a person, a Desolator. He is against the anointing of the most Holy.

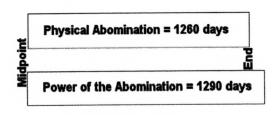

---

[16] Some people like to assign this "he" to the Roman general who destroyed Jerusalem's temple in 70 A.D. because it's "close enough" to the predicted date for the Messiah to be cut off around 32 A.D. and the close of the 70 sevens if there is no gap around 39 A.D. (see Appendix B). A failure to separate Luke 21 from the private Olivet Discourse further exacerbates this issue (see Appendix C).

[17] Though the term "antichrist" is not used here, the pattern of the previous abomination and the act of abomination itself lend themselves well to this term. The first defilement came at the hands of a person from history whose name is related, oddly enough, to the idea of an Antichrist—Antiochus Epiphanes, a name that means "instead of God revealed." The act of defiling the sanctuary is against anointing it or an anti-anointing. Christ simply means "anointed one." Hence, "Antichrist" is an appropriate term to describe the Desolator.

I know that these numbers can sometimes be difficult to follow, and I encourage you to again think through these things slowly and become familiar with the passages cited here.

By taking all this at face value, we see that there is a temple in Jerusalem that has a "Holy of holies" that will someday be defiled by the "Abomination of Desolation" by a Desolator. (While no temple currently exists in Jerusalem, this passage tells us that, sometime before or during the End Times, the temple will be rebuilt.) This Desolator, who is against the anointing of the temple, will defile it halfway through the last set of 70 sevens planned for Israel's punishment. This timeline is related to the end of the world (age) and the Second Coming, according to Jesus, and is related to six specific End-Times fulfillments for Israel, according to Daniel (Dan. 9:24). Twelve hundred and sixty days is a specific number that represents exactly one-half of a seven. Twelve hundred and ninety days points to a 30-day period after the "70 sevens."

By acknowledging the 30-day period after the 70th Seven, we can readily understand why Daniel stresses a time called the "consummation" in Dan. 9:27, a time needed to remove the one who caused the desolation. In the process of waiting for the "consummation," judgments decreed from God will "be poured upon the Desolator."

As we look for parallels, I find it interesting that the very last judgments recorded in the Revelation of Jesus Christ are also "poured out," and one is specifically poured on the "beast's throne" in Rev. 16:10. If we had the time and space, we could do a separate study that would tie together the "beast" with the "Antichrist" who desolates the temple.[18]

The desolation of the temple will end after 1,260 days from the midpoint of the last seven. The temple mount, Jerusalem, and her people will be holy, with prophecy being literally fulfilled as required by Dan. 9:24. The Desolator will not be in Jerusalem after that time. He will be cast out among the nations, waiting for

---

[18] Revelation 13 lays out pretty well that the beast is a man who utters blasphemes. This connects us to two of our other primary passages that deal with the Antichrist, 2 Thess. 2:3 and Dan. 11:36–12:1.

the 30-day consummation. Jerusalem will never again be his territory, nor be the trampling ground of the nations.

The last time the temple was desolated by an abomination, the one resulting in Hanukkah, it took about one week for the priests to purify and consecrate it. The End-Times Abomination of Desolation will remain in place for exactly 1,260 days, right up to the end of the 70th set of sevens, not leaving any time for a proper purification by priests. Revelation 11:2 says that Jerusalem will be "trampled by the gentiles [nations]" for 42 months. For those of you keeping score, 42 months of 30 days each equals 1,260 days. In other words, the Desolator and his ilk will have their "way" during this time. Both of these time periods, the desolation of the temple and the Desolator's total control of the city, have the same duration, and both will be abruptly ended, leaving no time for transition periods.

If there is no time for the priests to cleanse the temple; and day 1,261 is a fulfillment of all the prophecies to Israel in Dan. 9:24, including the anointing of the most Holy, then God must intervene to purify the temple. What has the ability to instantly vanquish any impurity? Only God's beautiful and utter holiness. Therefore, the Bible must speak of some event during which God exposes His holiness to impose it upon the defiled earthly temple to purify it. Could there be something in these six passages that suggests a method of instant purification? We shall soon see.

In summary, the Abomination of Desolation connects the Christians of Matthew 24, addressed as "you," and Daniel's "people and holy city," the Jews and Jerusalem. It is a future event, according to Jesus; and it is part of the 70 sevens, according to Daniel. All the time periods given spring forth from the abomination that is to occur at the middle of the last set of seven. Three time periods are given: 1,260 days, which is half of a seven, 1,290 days and 1,335 days. The 1,290 days is related directly to the Abomination of Desolation, while the 1,335 days is related to blessings. Daniel says that the "most holy" will be anointed after the 1,260 days. That means the Abomination of Desolation will be destroyed at that time. Because of the reference to the 1,290 days, however, we know that there are 30 extra days related to the Desolator who set up the abomination. At the end of those days, destruction will come upon the Desolator, the one we refer to as the Antichrist or "beast." And the language of judgments being "poured out" on him is eerily similar to the fifth bowl of Revelation as it is "poured out on the beast's throne."

The next connection will be very revealing. All we are looking for are similarities, parallels, dots to connect, the kinds of things you identify rather than concoct. As we patiently make more connections, we just might see a complete picture develop. Next, we will examine the events surrounding the end of the 70th Seven, connecting Daniel 9 and the seventh trumpet blast of the Revelation of Jesus Christ.

8

The Fulfillment of Promises

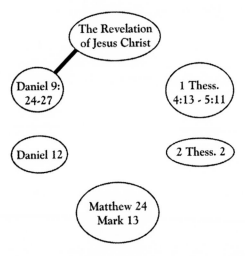

Daniel 9:24-27 ⇔ Revelation 10:7, 11:15, 11:19

Daniel 9:24–27 and Rev. 10:7, 11:15, 11:19 are two critical End-Times passages, and recognizing the link between them is the next logical step in following Jesus' example of putting two and two together. In this chapter, we will see that the six promises of Dan. 9:24 are fulfilled at the seventh trumpet.

Earlier in Chapter 9, Daniel had been praying because he knew that the 70 years of punishment declared by Jeremiah were near the end. Daniel longed for the nation to be restored and reconciled to God. Daniel received an answer from God that, yes, His relationship with Israel will be restored, and He gave six specific prophecies listed in Dan. 9:24 for the holy city and for

Israel. Once the seven times 70 years (or 70 sevens) of punishment elapsed, Daniel was told, the following six promises would become literal reality:

1. To finish the transgression.

The word translated "transgression" is *peh-shah*[19] in Hebrew. In this context, it refers to the kind of transgression that transpires at a national level, such as a collective moral or religious revolt against God's laws.

2. To make an end of sins.

The word translated "sins" is *khat-tawth*[20] and refers to habitual sinfulness, which required a penalty and the need for reconciliation and purification. This will be stopped.

3. To make reconciliation for iniquity.

The iniquity referred to here describes moral evil and the perverseness of a people group.[21] The promise is for God to forgive and reconcile with Daniel's people and Jerusalem.

4. To bring in everlasting righteousness (justice).

A new era will come to pass for the Jews and Jerusalem, one that will never end. This word translated "righteousness," *tseh-dek*,[22] encompasses the natural moral and legal order of things, resulting in perfect justice and equitable prosperity. I can't help but think of Daniel's vision in Daniel 2, in which God sets up an eternal kingdom.

5. To seal up the vision and prophecy.

Our phrase "seal up" here is the same Hebrew word translated earlier as "make an end."[23] At the end of this time, God will "close the books" on outstanding visions, dreams, revelations, and prophecies that will be fulfilled and the transactions completed. Keep in mind the context—that Daniel had been praying for God to restore the relationship with Israel.

---

[19] Strong's H6588; see Lev. 16:16, 21, Joshua 24:19, Jer. 5:6.
[20] Strong's H2403; see Gen. 18:20, Exodus 10:17 (habitual sin), and Exodus 29:36 (resulting in the need for an offering or to have a punishment taken away, as in the case with Pharaoh in Exodus 10:17).
[21] Strong's H5771, *awvone*, perversity, that is (moral) evil; see Gen. 15:16 or 19:15 and Jer. 30:14 for its application to a nation or city.
[22] Strong's H6664; see Lev. 19:15, 36 and Jer. 11:20.
[23] Strong's H2856, *khaw-tham*; see Isa. 29:11 and Jer. 32:10.

6. To anoint the most Holy.

This word "anoint" is *maw-shak*[24] in Hebrew. It is related to the word *maw-shee-akh*,[25] meaning "anointed one" or "messiah." It refers to a consecrated king or priest. The "most Holy" refers to a thing, which can be a person, place, or thing.[26] One can anoint the Holy of holies in the temple just as one can anoint a person, such as the Holy One of God, the Messiah.[27] Given the context of the list, either meaning (or even both together in an ultimate fulfillment) could be understood, given the conclusion of a time period resulting in an eternal reality.

Some would see these historically fulfilled by the Passion, Resurrection, and Pentecost. But this type of interpretation is a symbolic one. Though it could be argued that they were fulfilled in part, it is clear that they have yet to be fulfilled completely and literally, particularly for the "holy city." Foundationally, we know that these six promises must be fulfilled literally, for they are the final results of a series of events, each of which has already been fulfilled in history. The first prediction for the set of sevens was literally fulfilled when Jerusalem was rebuilt. The second prediction was also literally fulfilled when the Messiah was "cut off" (or killed). These two predictions completed the first 69 sets of seven. The last set of seven, therefore, awaits such promises as the completion of prophecy—reconciliation between God and Israel and the anointing of the Most Holy. Contextually, we have no choice, but to look forward to their literal fulfillment, as well.[28]

---

[24] Strong's H4886; see Exodus 28:41 and 30:26.

[25] Strong's H4899; see Psalm 18:50, Leviticus 4:5

[26] Strong's H6944, *kodesh*; see Exodus 3:5 (place), Exodus 15:11 (God), Exodus 15:13 (God's dwelling), Exodus 26:33-34 (the Holy of holies in the tent tabernacle where the ark of the covenant is), Exodus 28:2 (things), Psalm 2:6 (Mt. Zion).

[27] See Exodus 40:9-13, Num. 35:25, Psalm 89:20.

[28] Jesus did not fulfill all of these prophecies literally in the past in the same literal way that the other prophecies were fulfilled. We cannot pick and choose when we are going to take something literally and when we are not. If a series of events has a literal fulfillment, the next event in the sequence must be just as literal. Keep in mind, these promises are for Daniel's people and his holy city of Jerusalem.

It is clear from other portions of Scripture, such as Isaiah 65 and Zechariah 14, that Israel is awaiting such a fulfillment.

Therefore, what event could lead to the literal fulfillment of these promises? Would the Messiah reigning as King of kings, physically walking around on Mt. Zion, fulfill them? Would the one we call "Immanuel," which means "God with us," ruling with justice and mercy, solve the national waywardness of Israel? Given the extreme and ultimate nature of Dan. 9:24, only Israel's Messiah could bring permanent change. In other words, the Messiah's physical reign on earth is the only way to completely and literally fulfill the 70 sevens.

Daniel 9 and Revelation 10 and 11
Truly, such a turning point in world history, brought about by the Messiah, should be corroborated in a book claiming to be the revelation of that very Messiah. By looking for and recognizing common events, we can discover how events described in Revelation do, in fact, coincide with the literal fulfillment of events predicted at the close of the 70 sets of sevens in Daniel 9. Not only will we find that these events coincide, but we will see that both share the same ultimate significance as dividing lines in human history.

If both of these books predict the same grand transition in the plan of God, we need to sit up and take notice. Though each passage may use different words, the significance and results are identical. Daniel 9 and Revelation 10 and 11 share the most pivotal event in the history of man: the end of man's rule and the establishment of God's eternal kingdom on earth.

When Jesus sets up His everlasting earthly kingdom, He will simultaneously fulfill all six of the promises given in Dan. 9:24. Not only will He fulfill them, but He will do so permanently and literally in completion of prophecy. Consider the first four promises listed for Israel and Jerusalem. None of them have yet been completely fulfilled. Sin, war, and terror still pervade the region today; many who claim to be of Israel are faithless, and the idea of everlasting righteousness to them is a vapor or perhaps a childish hope. All the promises still await a future fulfillment.

Daniel 9	Revelation of Jesus Christ
9:24 Seventy weeks are determined upon thy people and upon thy holy city, ❶ to finish the transgression, ❷ and to make an end of sins, ❸ and to make reconciliation for iniquity, ❹ and to bring in everlasting righteousness, ❺ and to seal up the vision and prophecy, ❻ and to anoint the most Holy.	10:7 But in the days of the voice of the seventh angel, when he shall begin to sound, the mystery of God should be finished, as he hath declared to his servants the prophets. 11:15 And the seventh angel sounded; and there were great voices in heaven, saying, The kingdoms of this world are become the kingdoms of our Lord, and of his Christ; and he shall reign for ever and ever. 11:19 And the temple of God was opened in heaven, and there was seen in his temple the ark of his testament

Daniel 9	Revelation of Jesus Christ
1–3 finish national transgression/end habitual sinfulness/reconcile with Israel	11:19 Separation between God and man removed and the Ark of the Covenant is seen (Yom Kippur)
4 bring in everlasting righteousness	11:15 and he shall reign for ever and ever
5 seal up prophecy	10:7 Mystery of God finished as declared to prophets
6 anoint most Holy (where the Ark of the Covenant was kept)	11:15 Kingdoms of world become Christ's (Anointed One) 11:19 Ark seen in the Holy of holies in heaven!

Though Israel is the specific target of Daniel's prophecy, the fulfillment of these prophecies will affect the rest of the world by declaring an Israelite to be ruler of the world. Jesus is the "Lion of the tribe of Judah" (Rev. 5:5). By making good on the promises to Israel, God is making good on His promises to the world. He told Abraham that the whole world would be blessed through his offspring (Gen. 18:18). The fulfillment of the promises for "thy people" and "thy holy city" finds its alignment in the seventh trumpet blast of Revelation when Jesus takes authority over the nations. The king of Israel is the King of kings!

When all this happens at the seventh trumpet, the true Holy of holies, where God dwells in heaven, is opened and the Ark of the Covenant is exposed. Opening the heavenly temple and exposing the Ark of the Covenant is another way of saying that the Anointed One is reigning. All that the Ark of the Covenant represents, including God's mercy, atonement, and seat of authority, is literally fulfilled by God physically ruling on earth. Jesus is the embodiment of the Ark of the Covenant; and exposing it is exposing Jesus as the ruler of the world.

Furthermore, the contents of the Ark also find their alignment and ultimate fulfillment in Jesus Christ, the King of kings. First, there is the staff of Aaron that budded (Num. 17:8), which represents spiritual leadership. Second, there are the tablets of the Ten Commandments, which represent God's Word, the "Truth" (Exodus 31-34). And third, there is the pot of hidden manna, which represents God's provision (Exodus 16:32-34), the "Life." Jesus is "the Way, the Truth and the Life" (John 14:6).

Exposing the Ark of the Covenant in the Holy of holies means that God has ultimately fulfilled Yom Kippur, the Day of Atonement.[29] At this time, the Messiah is ruling in the capacity of Leader and Savior, and the promises at the end of the 70 sets of sevens are now a reality. The opening of the temple is the defining moment and the beginning of a whole new era of literal theocracy (God-run government). At the seventh trumpet, the end of the 70 sevens, the title deed and right to rule over the earth, including Israel, transfers from Satan to Jesus, thus beginning eternal righteousness and ending the punishment of Israel for their sin. Until the end of the 70 sevens and the seventh trumpet, Satan will remain the "god" of this world (2 Cor. 4:4).[30] But national reconciliation will begin with the 144,000 "first fruits" (the first of Israel to receive the promises)[31] on that day as they stand on Mt. Zion before the throne, as we see in Rev. 14:4.

---

[29] Yom Kippur is the sixth of seven feasts ordained by God in Leviticus 23. The Ark of the Covenant was only seen that day, once per year, and only then by the high priest.

[30] It should be noted the "beast"/Antichrist has ultimate authority for those last 1,260 days until his dominion is taken away. See Dan. 7:25–26 and Rev. 13:5. These time periods all spring out of the defilement of the temple at the midpoint of the 70th Seven.

[31] First Fruits is another Hebrew festival in the spring. It represents bringing to God the first fruits of the spring harvest as an offering in thanks for His provision. Many prophecy teachers add lots of deeds to the 144,000, calling them evangelists and what-not. The Bible calls them "first fruits," and we see Jesus presenting them to God in Rev. 14:1-4, right at the interval/interlude of the seventh trumpet/opening of the temple, when Jesus has begun to reign. These 144,000 from every tribe are the first to receive the promises: the nucleus of Israel. They will have a new song to sing to represent their new relationship.

How does all this relate to the Abomination of Desolation being instantly destroyed? When God's holy temple is opened and the Ark exposed, it is in the holiest of all places. Nothing—absolutely nothing—can withstand exposure to God's utter holiness if it is faulty. The Abomination of Desolation would cease to exist instantly. This is how the temple will be instantly purified exactly 1,260 days after its defilement. Let's take a moment to see how all this works.

According to Rev. 14:1–4, Jesus and the 144,000 are somehow simultaneously standing on Mt. Zion and before the throne in heaven at the same time. If we understand it simply, it would indicate that God's temple has invaded earth and makes Jerusalem holy, starting with a redeemed nucleus of 12,000 men from every tribe of Israel, literally fulfilling Dan. 9:24. This is how the six promises are not only fulfilled for Daniel's people, but for the holy city of Jerusalem, too.

This face-value understanding also explains the odd behavior of the people in Rev. 11:8–13. One minute, the people are rejoicing over the death of the Two Witnesses, reveling in their murder, and the next minute, they are glorifying God. There is only one thing that can do that—God's holiness experienced physically. Though these people may have hearts of stone, Luke 19:40 tells us that even the stones will cry out and shout "Hosanna." Just as the abomination shrinks away into oblivion by exposure to the Ark in the real heavenly Holy of holies, so is the attitude of men transformed in the immediate area.

Incidentally, this also explains why the battle of Armageddon occurs near Jerusalem and not in it or at a different locale. As Psalm 110 says, "he will rule in the midst of his enemies" and strike the kings through. The people will recognize the "beauty of his holiness." The nations that come to war will attempt to recapture Jerusalem. But just as Dan. 2:34–35 describes, God's kingdom is like a rock that expands into a mountain (Mt. Zion) and then consumes the whole earth.

In summary, the only way that the 70th Seven can be fulfilled to the point where Israel has a restored relationship with God, and with the holy city as a center of justice and righteousness, is for the Messiah to physically rule from Mt. Zion. We see this event transpire at the seventh trumpet in Revelation, where the fulfillment of these passages is the same as that listed in Dan. 9:24. Thus we see that the completion of the 70th Seven occurs at the seventh trumpet. Since Jesus is reigning literally from Mt. Zion, that means the Abomination of Desolation is gone. We also see an indication that the "Desolator" lives on after his Abomination of Desolation in Rev. 11:17–18, where the nations are enraged that Jesus has begun to reign.

Furthermore, the exposure of the true Ark of the Covenant in Rev. 11:19, and at the same time we see the intersection of heaven and earth on Mt. Zion as Jesus presents the 144,000 to God (Rev. 14:1–4), provides the means and proper timing for the instant removal of the Abomination of Desolation and for the "anointing of the most holy" at the end of the 70th Seven.

Putting the whole picture together, what we are seeing is a seven-year covenant with Israel where, midway through, the rebuilt Holy of holies is defiled and the city trampled by the nations. Both Israel and Christians ("you") are involved. Jesus tied the two together in Matthew 24 by giving us the example to follow. At the end of this last set of seven, all the promises of God to Israel will be instantly fulfilled to the day. The Church will have her Lord. Israel will have her Messiah. But for the world, there remains only judgment to consummate the new order.

So far, we have started with Jesus' example to connect Matthew 24 and the Daniel passages. Now we have seen how the Daniel passages align with events mentioned in the book of Jesus' Revelation. We should expect this in passages on the same topic, specific and inspired by the Holy Spirit. Perhaps it is time for us to come full circle in our connect-the-dots exercise.

Next, we will look at another direct connection between what Jesus is telling us in Matthew 24 and what He is showing us in His Revelation.

9

The Sun, Moon, and Stars

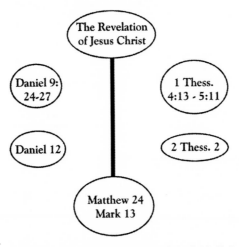

Matthew 24:29–31 ⇔ Revelation 6:11–7:1

To this point, we have had a chance to recognize a few obvious links. One is given to us by Jesus Himself as an example of how to unlock the order and sequence of the End Times. This allowed us to see how the Abomination of Desolation is related to the 70th Seven and the times of great tribulation about which Jesus taught in Matthew 24 and Mark 13. The other link gave us an intriguing parallel between the results of the seventh trumpet blast in the Revelation of Jesus Christ and the results of completing the 70 sets of seven in Dan. 9:24.

We now look to perhaps one of the most obvious similarities: the darkening of the sun, moon, and stars. Again, for many, it takes humility to draw this connection because their

teachers and seminaries may have taught them that there is no
connection here. My recommendation to you, the reader, is that we
continue to follow Jesus' example, compare the two passages,
stand back, and see if there are any further alignments. For if there
are further parallels and points of connection, we are only
continuing to unravel the mystery and expose the architecture of
End-Times prophetic events placed there by God. Rather than
fabricating reasons they shouldn't connect, we should just
acknowledge that they do.

Matthew 24	Revelation 6–7
24:29–31 ❶*Immediately after the tribulation of those days* shall the ❷<u>*sun be darkened, and the moon shall not give her light, and the stars shall fall from heaven,*</u> and the powers of the heavens shall be shaken: ❸*And then shall appear the sign of the Son of man in heaven:* ❹<u>*and then shall all the tribes of the earth mourn, and*</u> ❺*they shall see the Son of man coming in the clouds of heaven with power and great glory.* And he shall send his ❻*angels* with a great sound of a trumpet, and they shall gather together his elect from the ❼*four winds*, from one end of heaven to the other.	6:11–17 that they should rest yet for a little season, until their fellow servants also and their brethren, ❶*that should be killed as they were, should be fulfilled.* And I beheld when he had opened the sixth seal, and, lo, there was a great earthquake; ❷<u>*and the sun became black as sackcloth of hair, and the moon became as blood; And the stars of heaven fell unto the earth,*</u> even as a fig tree casteth her untimely figs, when she is shaken of a mighty wind. ❸*And the heaven departed [split apart—NASB] as a scroll when it is rolled together*; and every mountain and island were moved out of their places. ❹<u>*And the kings of the earth, and the great men, and the rich men, and the chief captains, and the mighty men, and every bondman, and every free man, hid themselves in the dens and in the rocks of the mountains; And said to the mountains and rocks, Fall on us,*</u> ❺*and hide us from the face [presence—NASB] of him that sitteth on the throne, and from the wrath of the Lamb.* 7:1... And after these things I saw four ❻*angels* standing on the ❼*four corners* of the earth, holding the ❼*four winds* of the earth...

The common denominator between Matthew 24 and
Revelation is, of course, Jesus. Just as in the case with the
previous connections, these two passages discuss very similar
signs, events, and sequences. One would hope that Jesus' teaching
during His earthly ministry would match up with the revelation He
gave to the Apostle John.

Let's look at each alignment in order:

❶ **Tribulation:** Both accounts begin with references to the martyrdom of Christians. In Matthew 24, the "tribulation of those days" is described earlier in the passage as "killing you...for my name's sake" (v. 9), as well as "the great tribulation" verse 21. Revelation describes those "slain for the Word of God and the testimony" during the fifth seal.

> For then there will be great tribulation, such as has not been since the beginning of the world until this time....(Matt. 24:21)

> ...that they should rest yet for a little season, until their fellow servants also and their brethren that should be killed as they were, should be fulfilled.... (Rev. 6:11)

❷ **Sun, moon, and stars:** In both accounts, the sun, moon and stars are darkened. The sun turns black, the moon's glow diminishes into a dark red, and the stars "fall" from the sky. This results in a complete blackening of the earth.

> Immediately after the tribulation of those days, the sun will be darkened, and the moon shall not give her light, and the stars shall fall from heaven, and the powers of the heavens shall be shaken. (Matt. 24:29)

> And I beheld when he had opened the sixth seal, and, lo, there was a great earthquake; and the sun became black as sackcloth of hair, and the moon became as blood; And the stars of heaven fell unto the earth, even as a fig tree casteth her untimely figs, when she is shaken of a mighty wind. (Rev. 6:12-13)

❸ **Sign of the Son of Man:** Immediately after the darkening of the light sources of the universe, something else happens in both accounts. Revelation describes it as the peeling back of the fabric of space. If the sky is being peeled back "like a scroll," then it must be exposing something other than the sky, something we've never seen before, perhaps something not of this universe. In Matthew 24, Jesus describes the same phenomenon, but in the Olivet Discourse, He is more specific because He is answering a question from the disciples: "What shall be the sign of thy coming?" Jesus tells them that, after the lights of the universe are darkened, something else will be visible: the sign of the Son of Man.

> And then shall appear the sign of the Son of man in heaven.... (Matt. 24:30)

> And the heaven departed [split apart, NASB] as a scroll when it is rolled together.... (Rev. 14)

❹ **All the tribes of the earth mourn:** In response to the cataclysmic events visible in the sky, everyone on the earth mourns at what they see. Revelation describes the people of the earth by their various stations in society, while Matthew 24 sums them up as the "tribes of the earth."

> ....and then shall all the tribes of the earth mourn (Matt. 24:30)

> And the kings of the earth, and the great men, and the rich men, and the chief captains, and the mighty men, and every bondman, and every free man, hid themselves in the dens and in the rocks of the mountains.... (Rev. 15–16)

In the Old Testament, a method of mourning was hiding and covering yourself with sackcloth and ashes. So utterly tragic is what the people of the earth see in the sky that they prefer mountains over ashes, preferring the mountains to fall on them and crush them in a suicidal fit of extreme mourning. Another reason to hide in the rocks and mountains is that this would block the extreme brilliance of what they are witnessing.

Isaiah 2 makes it clear that those who hide in the earth are hiding from God's glory:

> Enter into the rock, and hide thee in the dust, for fear of the Lord, and for the glory of his majesty. (Isa. 2:10)

> And they shall go into the holes of the rocks, and into the caves of the earth, for fear of the LORD, and for the glory of his majesty, when he ariseth to shake terribly the earth. (Isa. 2:19)

❺ **They shall see the Son of Man:** The sign of the Son of Man leads to actually seeing the Son of Man in His "power and great glory." That would surely be a very bright thing to see in contrast to a darkened universe!

> ...they shall see the Son of man coming in the clouds of heaven with power and great glory. (Matt. 24:30)

> And the kings of the earth, and the great men, and the rich men, and the chief captains, and the mighty men, and every bondman, and every free man, hid themselves in the dens and in the rocks of the mountains; And said to the mountains and rocks, Fall on us and hide us from the face [presence, NASB] of him that sitteth on the throne.... (Rev. 15–16)

Revelation describes the visible appearance of God on the throne with a reference to the Lamb, also known as the Son of Man. Jesus is "the brightness of his [God's] glory, and the express image of his person," according to Heb. 1:3. Jesus' face shines like the sun. Jesus is the Lamb of God, who is "in the midst of the throne" (Rev. 1:17, John 1:36, Rev. 7:17). In both accounts, the people of the earth are reacting to the impending "wrath of the Lamb," the second global judgment.[32]

❻ **Angels in the** ❼ **four winds:** Once the sign of the Son of Man is seen, God's messengers play an integral role in both accounts. They are going all over the place, to the four winds, actively accomplishing some task given to them by God. Matthew 24 tells us what that task is; Revelation 7 just shows us its result. They are gathering the righteous, those redeemed by Jesus from every, tribe, nation, and tongue.

> And he shall send his angels with a great sound of a trumpet, and they shall gather together his elect from the four winds, from one end of heaven to the other. (Matt. 24:31)

---

[32] We will examine this further in subsequent chapters.

> And after these things I saw four angels standing on the four
> corners of the earth, holding the four winds of the
> earth...These are the ones who come out of the great
> tribulation.... (Rev. 7:1, 14)

The table below summarizes how each of these passages
shares the same sequence:

Matthew 24	Revelation 6
Prelude: "Immediately after the tribulation..."	*Prelude:* Martyrdom of Christians (fellow servants)
Event: Sun, moon, stars darkened	*Event:* Sun, moon, stars darkened
Result: Everyone sees the Son...power and glory	*Result:* "Hide us from presence of him on throne and the wrath of the Lamb"
Angels: Angels gather elect from four winds	*Angels:* Angels work from four winds, two groups delivered

After comparing the two, it is quite obvious that they align.
A case for understanding the End-Times order and sequence is
building. Not only have we seen how the 70th Seven aligns with
the trumpet sequence, but now we are seeing apparently where the
blessed Rapture aligns with the seal events.

But, "Ah, ha!" you might say. "How can the Rapture occur
at the sixth seal if 'no one knows the day or hour'?" This is
perhaps one of the most misapplied scriptures on the End Times. If
you consider the context of this phrase (Matt. 24:36), you will see
that it sandwiched between admonishments by Jesus to look for
the season and recognize the times. By contrast, the "day or hour"
phrase has been used to suggest that the Rapture can happen at any
time, *regardless* of the season or the times.

Reread the context (Matt. 24:32–51). At face value, isn't
Jesus saying that when you recognize the season, the Rapture will
happen soon? And yet, knowing the season is not the same as
knowing the exact time. Just because we have probably identified
the Rapture occurring at the sixth seal doesn't mean that we know
the exact time it will take place. In fact, as our comparisons
continue to accumulate, we will see that this is just the case. If this
holds true, then the Rapture would neither start, occur midway
through, nor end the "Tribulation" (better described as the "70th
Seven"). Yes, it does appear that it takes place during the 70th

Seven, but its exact place within it is unknown. The season can be recognized, but the exact day or hour still can remain unknown.

But before we declare this dogmatically, we should make sure that the other Rapture passages align. We must be thorough and complete the picture. This leads us to the next logical connection: Matthew 24 and 1 Thess. 4:13–5:10.

10

Gathered Together: Caught Up

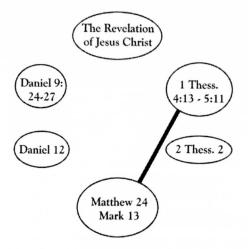

Matthew 24:30–33, 38–39, 42–43 ⇔ 1 Thessalonians 4:16–5:6

Thus far, we have followed Jesus' example by making connections at common points between texts on the End-Times. His pattern has allowed us to see the connections involving the Abomination of Desolation, the instant purification of the temple, and a period of consummation we associate with the extra 30 days. This led us to see the alignment between the completion of the 70 sets of seven, the seventh trumpet blast, and the beginning of Messianic rule. Then we continued by comparing the two instances involving the darkening of the sun, moon, and stars to see a probable connection to the Rapture at the sixth seal.

Now we come to the teaching of the Apostle Paul on the Rapture in 1 Thessalonians. Will it line up with the word of the Lord Jesus?

> For this we say unto you by the word of the Lord .... (1 Thess. 4:15)

Paul is explaining to his audience that he is only teaching them what the Lord Jesus taught on the subject. Was Matthew 24 the teaching that Paul was referring to? There is a good way to find out. We line up the two passages next to each other and look for commonalties, just as we did with the previous passages.

Matthew 24	1 Thessalonians
[30]And then shall appear the sign of the Son of man in heaven: and then shall all the tribes of the earth mourn, and they shall see the ❶ *Son of man* coming in the ❷ *clouds of heaven* with power and great glory. [31]And he shall send his angels with a great sound of a ❸ *trumpet*, and they shall ❹ *gather together* his elect from the four winds, from one end of heaven to the other. [32] ❺ *Now learn a parable of the fig tree; When his branch is yet tender, and putteth forth leaves, ye know that summer is nigh:* [33] *So likewise ye, when ye shall see all these things, know that it is near, even at the doors.* [38] ❻ *For as in the days that were before the flood they were eating and drinking, marrying and giving in marriage, until the day that Noe entered into the ark,* [39] *And knew not until the flood came, and took them all away;* ❼ *so shall also the coming of the Son of man be.* [42] ❽ *Watch therefore*: for ye know not what hour your Lord doth come. [43]But know this, that if the goodman of the house ❾ *had known in what watch the thief would come*, he would have watched, and would not have suffered his house to be broken up.	[16]For the ❶ *Lord himself* shall descend from heaven with a shout, with the voice of the archangel, and with the ❸ *trump* of God: and the dead in Christ shall rise first: [17]Then we which are alive and remain shall be ❹ *caught up together* with them in the ❷ *clouds*, to meet the Lord in the ❷ *air*: and so shall we ever be with the Lord. [18]Wherefore comfort one another with these words. [5:1] ❺ *But of the times and the seasons, brethren, ye have no need that I write unto you.* [2]For yourselves know perfectly that ❼ *the day of the Lord so cometh* as a ❾ *thief in the night.* [3] ❻ *For when they shall say, Peace and safety; then sudden destruction cometh upon them, as travail upon a woman with child; and they shall not escape.* [4] ❻ *But ye, brethren, are not in darkness, that that day should overtake you as a thief.* [5]Ye are all the children of light, and the children of the day: we are not of the night, nor of darkness. [6]Therefore let us not sleep, as *do* others; but let us ❽ *watch and be sober*.

Let's work through each of the connections in both passages to see if they hold.

❶ **Son of Man/Lord Himself:** Both accounts start by describing the visible appearance of Christ.

❷ **Heaven/air and "in the clouds":** Up in the sky is where these signs are appearing for all to see. Both terms refer to the sky. Clouds are often associated with the appearance of God or when heaven intersects earth. It may even be that, from our earthly perspective, heaven is cloud-like in appearance.

❸ **Great sound of a trumpet/the trump of God:** This event is heralded and announced by a loud trumpet call to action. The adjective "great" in Matthew 24 points to the special significance of this trumpet. In fact, it is the "trump of God" rather than a trumpet blown by an angel. During the Second Coming, God will be physically intervening in the affairs of man, just as He did in the First Coming.

❹ **Gather together/caught up together:** Believers are Raptured to be with the Lord. They leave the earth to be with the Lord up in the clouds of the heavenly realm.

❺ **Season of spring to summer/times and seasons**: Trees bud in the spring and are fully leafed in the summer. These times and seasons are to be obvious to the audience (Christians). We will not be surprised at their suddenness as we would by a thief randomly coming in the night. We will be able to recognize the season of Christ's return and be prepared.

❻ **Marrying, then the Flood came/safety, then destruction:** The second global judgment will follow same pattern as first one during the Flood of Noah. The "dwellers of the earth" will go on about their lives, oblivious to the signs and will be taken off-guard and destroyed.

❼ **Coming of the Son of Man/Day of the Lord comes:** The suddenness of the coming of our God is equated to the suddenness of the destruction of the global judgments. The Day of the Lord and the Rapture are contextually lumped together. Some people recognize this, but go to the extreme, forcing these events to occur all at the same moment. Others recognize their different functions, but go the opposite extreme of separating them into two different comings. The truth is that the Greek word we translate into "coming," *parouisa*, is a noun, and it implies many actions,

deeds, and comings and goings over a period of time.[33] The First
Coming lasted for over 30 years; the Second Coming will begin at
the Rapture and continue through the Millennium and forever.

❽ **Watch and be sober:** Be vigilant so that you do not fall
into a slumber of living in the world and being caught off-guard by
the return of the Lord. The current man-centered system will be
suddenly uprooted.

❾ **Thief in the night:** The suddenness of the Second
Coming and global judgments are just like the suddenness of a
thief who breaks into your house in the middle of the night when
you least expect it to attack you and destroy your life.

Paul had an opportunity to write a second letter to the
Thessalonians that further expounds upon the End-Times topic
with sequences and details. Are we asking too much to see further
parallels?

---

[33] *Parousia*, Strong's G3952, is a noun we narrowly translate into English
as "coming," but it has a richer meaning that includes "advent" and "a
near presence." I doubt a Greek would use this word to describe
somebody who suddenly pops in and then pops out. It was used to
describe significant visits by the king, who would be accessible to the
people and spend time with them. It would include many acts and deeds.
Jesus' First Coming is a perfect example of this.

11

Order and Sequence

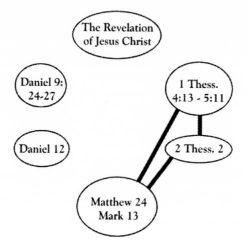

Matthew 24:30–31, 38–39, 42–43 ⇔ 1 Thessalonians 4:16–5:3

⇔ 2 Thessalonians 2:1–3, 6

2 Thessalonians 2 is a key passage in placing the pieces together. It contains some very explicit ordering of End-Times events. It is imperative that we know whether the sequence given by Paul is meant to be something for the Church to witness before the Rapture or whether this teaching is purely academic and corrective.

According to 2 Thess. 2:2, the young church in Thessalonica had come under the misunderstanding that perhaps their severe sufferings were the result of God's wrath. Their trials were so severe, in fact, that they thought they might have missed the Rapture and were living in the Day of the Lord about which Paul had taught in the previous letter. Paul attempts to set the record straight by first creating a list of three events—the coming, descending, and arrival of Jesus; the gathering together of the Church; and the suddenness of the Day of the Lord (or Day of Christ) to inflict wrath—followed by a sequence of events that must occur before the Day of the Lord begins.

But the question has always been "before what?" Is Paul talking about before the Day of the Lord only? Or before all three events? If Paul meant to separate these events, he did a poor job. If Paul had meant to group all three together, this is a good way to do it. He was already addressing people who were familiar with his previous letter and teachings. He really only needed to mention the three events he wished to clarify in his opening sentence. Verses one and two are all part of the same sentence and thought. This is the most customary and plain sense way to understand written communication. We are to get our understanding by reading out of the text rather than imposing our ideas into it. It is the desire to make the Rapture occur before the sequence given here by Paul that has caused the confusion.

The resolution goes back to the issue of whom Jesus is addressing in Matthew 24. Who is the "you" that will be hunted down and live to see the abomination, with the opportunity to flee? Is the "you" the Church or Israel only? If it's the Church, then Christians will live to see the abomination and live through a period of great trial, sometimes called "the Great Tribulation" (verse 21). If it is Israel only, then dare we say that Matthew spent an inordinate amount of space telling future Christians about what Israel will see and do during these days that Christians would never see? Which one is the simple, face-value understanding?

A step in getting there is to determine whether these three passages have any parallels. If Paul is truly just passing on what Jesus taught, then we should expect to see a similar order between them. And if they align, and if 2 Thessalonians 2 speaks of a sequence of events involving the temple abomination just as Jesus gave in His example, we should definitely take note.

The following chart compares the three passages:

Matthew 24	1 Thessalonians	2 Thessalonians
24:30–31 And then shall appear the sign of the Son of man in heaven: and then shall all the tribes of the earth mourn, and they shall see the ❶ *Son of man coming in the clouds* of heaven with power and great glory. And he shall send his angels with a great sound of a trumpet, and they shall ❷ *gather together his elect* from the four winds, from one end of heaven to the other. 24:38–39 ❸ *For as in the days* that were before the flood they were eating and drinking, marrying and giving in marriage, *until the day* that Noe entered into the ark, And knew not until *the flood came, and took them all away; so shall also the coming of the Son of man be.* 24:42–43 Watch therefore: for ye *know not what hour your Lord doth come. But know this,* that if the goodman of the house had known in *what watch the thief would come...*	4:16 – 5:3 ❶ *For the Lord himself shall descend from heaven with a shout*, with the voice of the archangel, and with the trump of God: and the dead in Christ shall rise first: Then ❷ *we which are alive and remain shall be caught up together with them in the clouds, to meet the Lord* in the air: and so shall we ever be with the Lord. Wherefore comfort one another with these words. But of the times and the seasons, brethren, ye have no need that I write unto you. For yourselves know perfectly that the ❸ *day of the Lord so cometh as a thief in the night. For when they shall say, Peace and safety; then sudden destruction.*	2:1–3 Now we beseech you, brethren, by the ❶ *coming of our Lord Jesus Christ*, and by ❷ *our gathering together unto him,* That ye be not soon shaken in mind, or be troubled, neither by spirit, nor by word, nor by letter as from us, as that the ❸ *day of Christ* is at hand. Let no man deceive you by any means: for *that day shall not come, except...* 2:6 Seeing it is a righteous thing with *God to recompense tribulation to them* that trouble you.

Without even looking at the context, we see that the order of events is rigidly the same. In all three passages, the following order is maintained:

- First, the coming, descending, and arrival of Jesus.
- Second, the gathering together of the Church.
- Third, the suddenness of the Day of the Lord/Christ to inflict wrath.

This is enough for us to see that they may actually speak of the same events. In fact, we would have to impose a bias, outside of the Bible, to arrive at any other conclusion. What else do these passages share?

Matthew 24 and 2 Thessalonians 2 both mention the abomination in the temple in Jerusalem. Jesus told His audience to watch out for the abomination spoken of by Daniel and flee when they see it. Daniel elaborates on this abomination, explaining that it is caused by a person midway through the last set of 70 sevens and that this person will declare himself as "god" (Dan. 11:36). 2 Thessalonians 2 also specifically points to a person who abominates the temple in Jerusalem by declaring himself to be "god." This Desolator will show up before the Second Coming, which Paul describes in verse 1.

Is it a coincidence that they mention the same events? Is it a coincidence that all these passages tie together and relate on a fundamental level, requiring minimal bias from us? Can we further expand our links to include the sixth seal of Revelation when we have already seen how Jesus' coming aligns with Matthew 24 and 1 Thessalonians?

In 2 Thessalonians, the Day of the Lord (the wrath of God against the wicked world), is termed the *Day of Christ*. It is another way of saying the "Day of the Lord," with special focus on the actions of Jesus Christ. The sixth seal also gives us special emphasis on another event: *the wrath of the Lamb*, as opposed to the more usual term "the wrath of God." Both are said to be *at hand*, and both provide another connection at a critical junction where the Rapture by Jesus is seen to occur.

We don't need to force things to see how they tell their own story. In accordance with the Great Commission, the "you" of Matthew 24 is directed first at the disciples, then at Paul, then at the Thessalonian believers, then at the church to the present and to the time of the end. Christians of the future are to watch for a time when love grows cold and for the Abomination of Desolation as an indicator of the season of the Great Tribulation that will be suddenly ended when Christians are Raptured away.

We are beginning to see how Matthew 24, Daniel 9, Daniel 12, and 2 Thessalonians are connecting at the defilement of the temple and apostasy. The alignments continue at many levels. Is it bias or the recognition of a plan already there?

The time of the Great Tribulation and the events leading up to it can further be connected by another common analogy used by Paul and Jesus—the birth pangs. But before we get there, the next chapter looks to see if the events mentioned by Jesus in Matthew 24 line up with the seals of Revelation.

12

Seals and Sorrows

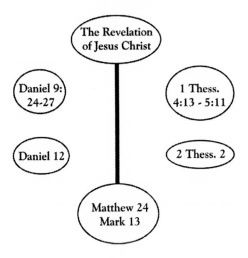

Matthew 24:5–8, 15, 29, 39 ⇔ The Revelation of Jesus Christ 6, 8:1

Do the birth pangs in Matthew 24 line up with the seals in Chapter 6 of Revelation? Again, we are looking at aligning passages that speak of similar events on the surface so as to minimize our imposed bias. By following this method, we have seen how all these specific texts on the topic parallel.

The table below compares the two passages:[34]

---

[34] For the sake of brevity, I've abbreviated Matthew 24 to M24.

Revelation of Jesus Christ		Matthew 24
Seal 1: Conqueror (Antichrist)	Rev. 6:1 = M24:5	**Event 1:** False christs
Seal 2: Global war	Rev. 6:3 = M24:6	**Event 2:** Global wars
Seal 3: Food shortages	Rev. 6:5 = M24:7	**Event 3:** Famines and disease
Seal 4: Combo of the first three with consequences of physical and spiritual death *"killing with hunger"*	Rev. 6:7 = M24:8	**Event 4:** Tribulation and martyrdom with instructions and warnings to the disciples of Christ – Beware of spiritual deception!
Seal 5: Martyrs under the altar, waiting for their number to be full	Rev. 6:9 = M24:15,22	**Event 5:** Flee; God will cut short the time
Seal 6: Sun, moon, stars/deliverance	**Rev.** 6:12 = M24:29	**Event 6:** Sun, moon, stars/deliverance
Seal 7: Destruction of the wicked and world	**Rev. 8:1=** M24:39	**Event 7:** Destruction of the wicked and world

I hope that you are going back to these above referenced scriptures and comparing them with each other to see the points of connection for yourself. Those who would prefer to separate these two scriptures, which are both on the same topic and find their source in the same person, into separate events will certainly be accountable to the Lord. It doesn't take rocket science or special knowledge to see how they align.

Now let's look at each event in more detail:

The first event compares two "savior" appearances. In Matthew 24,[35] Jesus tells the four disciples to watch out for false saviors, while the first seal reveals a white rider with a laurel crown typical of a savior/victor of the Roman Empire. Some have claimed that this Roman image of the white rider is Jesus Himself (see Rev. 19:11–16), while ignoring the fact that a laurel is not the same as a regal diadem crown. Olympic champions wore laurels. Kings wear crowns. Moreover, this white rider carries a bow, while Jesus needs no bow.

---

[35] Some people call the seals "judgments." While they are not judgments in the sense of condemnation, they can be seen as judgments in the sense described by Eze. 14:21 and 1 Peter 4:17.

The truth, I believe, requires less imagination and better observation. The imagery would have been very familiar to the disciple John, who wrote Revelation, as he lived during the Roman Empire, where triumphal processions hailed the champions of Rome. The crowds would line the streets and shout wonderful things at the victor wearing the laurel, even to the point that the champion might believe he was a god worthy of god-like attention. Traditionally, the Romans had counter-measures to make sure that the person being hailed did not seek to take the place of Caesar, who was a god in their minds. All the while, a slave would stand behind the victor, whispering into his ear that glory was fleeting.

Hmmm, now where does this idea of a conquering victor who is imitating God come into play? The comparison of the "white rider" to the White Rider of Rev. 19:11–16 is more significant when we take into account both the similarities and the mutually exclusive differences, particularly the type of crown worn. The Antichrist is against the anointing of the temple. "Antichrist" means "against the anointed one" (see the footnote on in Chapter 7). The Antichrist plans on declaring himself as "god" and "savior" in place of our Lord. He is seen as riding the white horse, just as Jesus will at Armageddon. He is seen sitting on the throne (the tabernacle, the Ark of the Covenant), which is reserved for Jesus when He rules the world. The Antichrist will set up a kingdom, an extension of empires that Jesus will destroy with His own eternal kingdom formed by the hand of God rather than by the hands of men (Dan. 2:34, 45). He will put marks on his people to seal them, just as God marks His own and seals them with the Spirit (Rev. 13:16, 14:1, Eph. 4:30). He will overcome his enemies, the saints, just as Jesus will return and put all things into submission to God (Rev. 13:7, 19, 1 Cor. 15:24–26). The Antichrist will play a role in an unholy tri-pact, whereas Jesus is the Son of God, second person of the holy, triune God.

Putting it all together, this rider is not Jesus Christ. He is the Antichrist, the imitator of Christ. Jesus will be the Faithful and True rider at Armageddon, not just someone claiming truth and good faith. He will be the King of kings at Armageddon, not just a conquering leader. He will wear diadem-style crowns of a ruler rather than the victor's headpiece of athletic events. In addition to the fact that the Antichrist will commit all these "anti-deeds," it is inappropriate to view Christ as the rider when He is the one opening the seals. The white rider is one in a series of riders. Jesus is not one in a series of anything. He is the one and only!

The reason this is such an important point is that this first event signifies the beginning of the last seven. The "Tribulation," or more appropriately the "70th Seven," begins right here. This understanding goes back to Dan. 9:27, when this "he," identified as the Antichrist, upholds a seven-year treaty with "many," relating to Jerusalem and her people. A false savior with good intentions shows up to deceive many.

With this, we should be able to construct a basic timeline for the 70th Seven, for now we know its beginning, midpoint, and end. The 70th Seven begins with the false savior showing up to enforce a multi-national, seven-year pact with Israel for peace in the Middle East. At the exact midpoint, the false savior wants to be the real Savior. It all technically ends for this usurper when the seventh trumpet announces the transfer of authority to the One who really is Faithful and True.

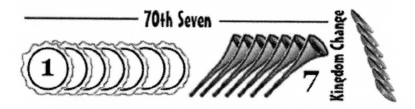

So this Antichrist begins by deceiving and conquering through peace. He may be revered as the Messiah.[36] Yet, while he conquers in peace, he carries a bow, a weapon of war.

---

[36] Briefly, the teachers of Israel have always known that the Messiah would be a conqueror and a suffering servant. What they did not know is that these two different aspects would be fulfilled separately over thousands of years. While under the oppression of the Roman Empire, they longed for the Messiah to come and free them from oppression, so much so that they missed recognizing Him as the suffering servant and killed Him. The Messiah came first as the Passover Lamb to "reconnect" man to God, to rekindle the life in man's spirit. Without first dealing with man's dead spirit, it would be pointless to perpetuate man's corrupted

The second event aligns with war and bloodshed. Wars are the inevitable result of conquering those who resist. When Jesus conquers at Armageddon, there is no battle. The armies of the world simply die at His command. So, again, we see that the white rider's identity appears to be one of deception. It will be something like, "I come in peace, and if you don't like it, then I will *make* you at peace with me."

The third event aligns with the collateral damage. Famines are the inevitable result of wars. Infrastructures are destroyed, preventing the delivery of goods and services to the populations. The black rider epitomizes these food shortages in the war-torn areas of those who resist.

The fourth event, expressed as the pale rider, is really about two riders. The pale rider is called "Death." We think of him as the Grim Reaper, the one who brings physical death. But what else does this passage say? Power was given to "them" (plural) to kill. "Hell, or more properly rendered "Hades,"[37] is the second rider who follows. It is this dynamic duo that spans one-quarter of the globe using these things to kill. One represents physical death and the other spiritual death. This aligns with Jesus' description of persecutions and His warnings to avoid spiritual deceptions in Matt. 24:9–11.

---

state into an everlasting kingdom ruled by the Source of Life. By "cutting off" the Anointed One (Messiah), God has extended His grace beyond the children of Abraham to the rest of the world, the children of Noah. As a result, the 69th Seven was completed by the First Coming of the Messiah; then a gap called the "Time of the Gentiles" ensued, during which all nations have been blessed as a result of Abraham's faith. "Have they stumbled that they should fall? God forbid: but rather through their fall salvation is come unto the Gentiles, for to provoke them to jealousy" (Romans 11:11). If we get down to brass tacks, modern Jewish rabbis will deny any connection of the Messianic prophecies to Jesus. They have even gone so far as to attribute the Messianic passages of Isaiah to text-meddling by zealous Christians. With this kind of bias, is it any wonder that they have set themselves up for the Great Deception?

[37] Hades is a temporary abode for the damned dead that exists as long as the fallen universe exists. It will be thrown into the Lake of Fire, also known as hell, for eternity before the new heavens and new earth are realized. See Rev. 20:14.

The fifth event correlates with the mounting numbers of martyrs, those who chose physical death rather than spiritual death. Only God knows when that number will be fulfilled here in the fifth seal, just as only God knows when this time will be cut short (Matt. 24:22).[38] Only God knows the day and the hour of the sixth seal rescue.

The sixth event has already been extensively reviewed in an earlier link. The deliverance and rescue of the suffering believers comes "immediately after the tribulation of those days" when the signs in the sky are given, according to Matt. 24:29 and following. The "Rapture" occurs and God protects His own just before He begins to judge the world.

And lastly, in **the seventh event**, before the rest of the world can rub out of their eyes what they have seen, the second global judgment will arrive quickly, seizing the world in a series of trumpet-blast judgments. Back in Matthew 24, Jesus warns us that these times will be just like the times of the Flood when people thought the way things were would just continue on, until suddenly they were swept away.

It is clear that these two passages align in more than one way. Jesus refers to the first few events as "the beginning of sorrows" or "birth pangs" that naturally lead up to the travail of hard labor and birth of the last few events.

The next chapter will look at this analogy, employed also by the Apostle Paul, to see if it can lend any assistance to us in understanding the sequences of the 70th Seven.

---

[38] Either the Antichrist will succeed in eradicating the elect before the end of the last seven or he may succeed in making all flesh bear his mark, or likely both. How far God will let this go so that one other person can be saved may someday be up to you. Is all the temporary suffering of many comparable to the value of one soul?

13

The Birth Pangs Pattern

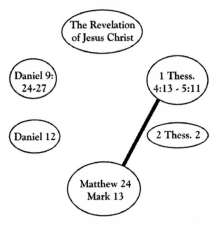

Matthew 24:8 1 ⇔ Thessalonians 5:3

There is an *ante-partum* ward in some hospitals where they work hard at preventing premature birth, for everyone knows that once the process of labor begins, it results in delivery. It's not as if the expectant mother can stop the birth pangs by willing them to subside. I know this as a husband and father many times over. During labor, the pain increases with each new wave of pangs. When they first start, you know that the clock has started ticking. The closer the mother gets to the time of childbirth, the shorter the intervals between each labor pang. At the point of birth, there is very little time between each contraction.

Jesus (Matt. 24:8) and Paul (1 Thess. 5:3) both use the example of birth pangs to describe the cascading events of the future. The analogy, taken at face value, is that these events will start slowly and then speed up into hard labor. The interval between each contraction is less in duration and more severe as birth draws closer. This implies that the time between the opening of each seal is less and less.

It is the fourth seal that really starts to get serious for Jesus' followers. This is the point in the sequence at which the birth pangs turn into hard labor. Jesus is explicit as He describes this break in Matt. 24:8–9. From that point on, Jesus describes suffering and martyrdom. In accordance with our alignments from the previous chapter, the fourth and fifth seals are referred to by Jesus as the "tribulation of those days" (Matt. 24:29).

To help us understand the beginning of hard labor and the tribulation of those days, Jesus sends us to Daniel (Matt. 24:15) so we can understand the source of this tribulation—the Desolator who sets up the Abomination of Desolation—so that we can be watchful for the season. The birth pangs begin with the deception of the white rider. The difficult times continue to increase with war and famines to the point that the persecutions resulting from the abomination take over at the midpoint of the 70th Seven.

Thus, we see that the third seal brings food shortages, and these shortages are being used as a tool of coercion in the fourth seal. This choice between physical and spiritual death will correspond to the time that the saints are faced with the decision between worshiping the beast and accepting his mark (spiritual death) or being killed (Revelation 12, 13, 14). Those who take the mark will suffer the consequences of Hades, leading to the Lake of Fire. Those who refuse will do so as a result of their faith in Jesus will accept physical death and join the ranks of the fifth seal martyrs under the altar. This is all related to the Abomination of Desolation when the deceiver declares himself to be "god," sitting in the Holy of holies.

Therefore, we can know that the fourth seal begins sometime *after* the midpoint of the 70th Seven, but how close to the midpoint we cannot know with exactness. It could be the severe food shortages of the third seal that finally pave the way for the Antichrist (or Desolator) to set up shop in the temple in Jerusalem. It could be the lack of opposition that allows this man of lawlessness to break his treaty. Those likely not to be fooled (the Christian world) comprise approximately one-quarter of the earth and will need a little "encouragement." In any case, the midpoint of the 70th Seven is likely to occur between the third and fourth seals.

Now we can construct a basic outline of the 70th Seven that begins with the first seal and ends with the seventh trumpet blast. Working from the rear, we know that there are seven trumpet blasts that all fit into the second half of the 70th Seven. We know the third and fourth seals straddle the midpoint and that the interval between each consecutive seal is less and less.

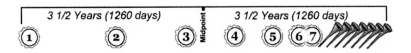

When the birth pangs start, we cannot predict the exact time of birth; we can only recognize that the time has come. We can know the season and the times, but we cannot know the day or the hour of Jesus' return. Both timing aspects of the Rapture are completely satisfied by taking all of these passages in their usual and customary sense. The pre-tribbers and the post-tribbers are both right and wrong. One group focuses on recognizing the seasons and the other on not knowing the day or the hour. Jesus spoke of both at the same time. Both views can be satisfied in this scheme. The seasons, and even the very first and last days, of the 70th Seven can be known while the exact day and hour of the Rapture remains unknown.

It is when people take passages that are not on the topic and insert their own preconceived notions into them, and then turn around and use those off-topic passages to define those passages that *are* on the topic, that you get confusion. The passages that we looked at earlier, James 5:7-9 and 1 Cor. 15:51-52, are prime examples of this. Both of these passages and others used by pre-tribbers and post-tribbers are not focused on discussing the End Times. Proponents of these views are using them to make their own End-Times "house of doctrine" with broomsticks and cardboard. Aren't the results amazing when we get our understanding of a topic from passages that are actually *discussing* the topic?

In the next chapter, we will see that Revelation and Matthew also discuss times of unknown duration and that they stand in stark opposition to the specific "to the day" periods of time given elsewhere.

14

The 'Short Times' Link with Perseverance

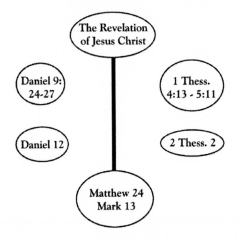

Matthew 24:22, 32, 38 ⇔ Revelation 6:11, 12:12

In this chapter, we'll take a look at some of the time periods in End-Times scripture for which there is an unknown duration. These times are spoken of in two of our primary group scriptures and are referred to as:

- No one knows the day or hour (Matt. 24:38).
- The season of summer drawing close (Matt. 24:32).
- The times will be cut short (Matt. 24:22).
- A little while until their number is complete (Rev. 6:11).
- The Devil's great wrath is only for a short time (Rev. 12:12).

- The patience (perseverance) of the saints (Rev. 13:10, 14:12).

Let's start with Rev. 12:12:

...for the Devil is come down unto you, having great wrath, because he knoweth that he hath but a short time. (Rev. 12:12)

The "Devil's great wrath" is a result of the "short time" given him to complete his deception of man. During this time, Satan will pull no punches. He will go for it all. He will bring to bear all of his evil devices to deceive the nations while he can.

The parallels continue to mount as we compare scripture with scripture. This "short time" allotted for the "Devil's great wrath" coincides with the "shortening" of the Great Tribulation for the sake of the elect (Matt. 24:22) and the "little season" only known by God when the number of martyrs will be complete (Rev. 6:11). These "short" time periods are markedly undefined compared to the more precise time periods such as the 42 months or 1,260 days.

The obvious nature of a short time, or a shortened time, is that no one knows when the time is up. It is a time period that has been shortened from another time period that has likely been stated or previously set. These "short times" agree and find their beginning at the midpoint of the 70th set of seven. God, the Father, will determine when these "short times" are up by telling Jesus it is time for Him to harvest the earth by gathering the saints and treading the winepress of wrath out to its necessary conclusion.[39] None of this is meant to be a mystery.

Behold, I have told you before. (Matt. 24:25)

All these shortened times contain a common theme: the perseverance of the saints. It is this theme that confirms our simple understanding of Matthew 24 as being directed to Christians. Even the context of Paul's famous Rapture passage in 1 Thessalonians is

[39] In Rev. 14:14–20, God dispatches an angel to tell Jesus it is time to reap.

written to a church, requiring patience in trials as they look forward to the appearing of our Lord (1 Thess. 1:10, 3:3, 13, 2 Thess. 1:4–10).

The book of Revelation is no exception. It is written to those "who have an ear in the churches" in chapters 2 and 3. The implication is that not everyone will have an ear; it will fall to individual overcomers to remain faithful. Terms such as "elect" and "saints" and "those who hold to the testimony of Jesus" would be appropriate to describe the individual faithful believers within the Church rather than the Church corporately. A general apostasy (2 Thess. 2:3, Matt. 24:10, 12) and persecution that erodes the corporate structure would result in a situation that requires individuals to become overcomers.

> And then shall many be offended, and shall betray one another, and shall hate one another...because iniquity shall abound, the love of many shall wax cold. (Matt. 24:10, 12)

The church at Smyrna is told that they will endure tribulation 10 days and exhorted to be faithful unto death (Rev. 2:10). The church at Thyatira has those who may suffer even more than those of Smyrna during the tribulation in order that they may be purified of their immorality (Rev. 2:22). The church at Philadelphia has those who have "kept the word of My patience [perseverance]" (Rev. 3:10).

What is this patience (perseverance) of the saints? How does it relate to the suffering at the hands of the beast?[40]

> Here is the patience and the faith of the saints. (Rev. 13:10)

> Here is the patience of the saints: here are they that keep the commandments of God, and the faith of Jesus. (Rev.14:12)

The context of these two passages refers directly to those who stand firm against the beast and his system (Revelation 13). These saints do not worship the beast's image or take the beast's mark. The whole earth will be deceived, and those who are not written in the Lamb's Book of Life will worship the beast. This

---

[40] See discussion and footnotes in Chapter 7.

beast will make war with the saints and overcome them (Rev. 13:7, Dan. 7:21). "Overcoming" means they will be killed because they refuse to worship the beast's image. The saints will take the physical consequences of death over the spiritual consequences of Hades as we see in the fourth seal.

Is it starting to make sense why Jesus would tell the disciples to flee the area when they see the abomination?

The fifth seal martyrs are those who die because they do not worship the image of the beast or take his mark. They are all described as keeping the Word of God and their witness for Jesus intact (Rev. 6:9). It is no small wonder that those who are "alive and remain" at Christ's return (1 Thess. 4:15) need comforting because of the horrors they have been through. They come straight out of the Great Tribulation (Rev. 7:14–16), as the elder told John. This tribulation is not inflicted by God but by the Devil and the men who serve his system.[41] As the deaths of his saints begin to mount, their cry grows louder and louder from beneath the altar in the most Holy place before God's throne in heaven during the fifth seal. When their number is complete (the sixth seal), God answers their prayers (the seventh seal) and brings justice swiftly (the trumpets and the bowls). The exact timing is only known by God, the Father.

It is the Devil who sets up the system for global worship of the beast's image. It is the Devil who forces people to take the beast's mark to be able to participate in the economy. The Great Tribulation is a direct result of this global system of man, "great Babylon,"[42] in which its leader exalts himself above all others, just as the historical king of Babylon did in the book of Daniel.[43] That self-aggrandizing king threw God's servants into the fiery furnace while the future leader may do that and more. Even biblical

---

[41] God is not inflicting or causing the suffering. He is allowing it to purify the bride of Christ. Remember, the temporary suffering of many leads to righteousness and allows for more to believe. Only God knows when that last person will receive Christ before He turns the tides and removes the remaining saints to begin His wrath. Who will be that overcoming saint who lays down his life for his future friend in heaven?

[42] Revelation 14:8, 16:19, 17:5, 18:2, 10, 21.

[43] Daniel 4:30 and his all gold image of Daniel 3.

accounts such as Daniel in the lion's den reveal a pattern of individual suffering and deliverance by God.

The point is that suffering will occur to purify the Bride of Christ (1 Peter 4:17, Eph. 5:27) and complete the punishment of Israel.[44] For Israel, we know the exact timing; for the Church, we do not. These undefined times are not to confuse us, but they exist as a testimony of love from God to us. The 42 months have been shortened out of love for us.

> ...but for the elect's sake those days shall be shortened. (Matt. 24:22)

Jesus, the Bridegroom, will come to take away His "spotless," tried and true Bride to the marriage supper. The 144,000 of Israel will be supernaturally preserved through it all to become the first of those who would believe and receive the fulfilled promises of God to Israel.[45] The sequence of the 70th Seven is now coming into focus.

Daniel 70th Seven Dan 9:24-27

In summary, these undefined short times speak to the time before the Rapture. They represent, primarily, a segment of the second half of the 70th Seven. Only God knows how much of the second half these comprise. Working backwards from the end, we know from the duration of some of the trumpet judgments,

---

[44] The completion of the 70th Seven will complete the seven times seventy punish for Israel.

[45] They saw Egypt's army drowned at the Red Sea crossing. They witnessed Assyria's army being slaughtered by an angel during Elijah's time. Now they will see an even greater thing.

particularly the fifth (Rev. 5:9), that the maximum duration of these short times is about three years.

As the primary passages continue to sharpen our focus on the order of End-Times events, we realize that the bowl judgments are not yet in sight. In the next section, we will look at the purpose and timing of the bowls. We will see why the bowl judgments must occur within a period of time of 30 days or less.

15

The Bowl Judgments — 30 Days

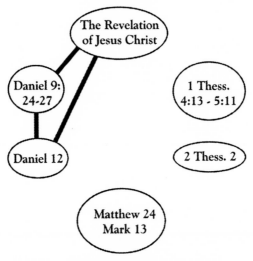

Daniel's extra 30 days from the midpoint ⇔

The Revelation of Jesus Christ 15–19

We now come to our last major link in developing a cohesive doctrine of the End Times based upon simple connections. Some of them are initially more obvious than others; while some, like this one, require additional study of the passages. For we know that Daniel has laid out additional periods of time that extend beyond the 70th Seven.

> From the time that the regular sacrifice is abolished and the abomination of desolation is set up, there will be 1,290 days. (Dan. 12:11, NASB)

We've seen how the Holy of holies is to be defiled for exactly one-half of the 70th Seven.

> And he shall enter into a strong and firm covenant with many for one week [seven years]. And in the midst of the week he shall cause the sacrifice and offering to cease [for the remaining three and one-half years]; and upon the wing or pinnacle of abominations [shall come] one who makes desolate, until the full determined end is poured out on the desolator. (Dan. 9:27, Amplified)

This Desolator is against the anointing. He is the Antichrist. The Desolator and the desolation are different. Whereas the desolation is destroyed at the end of the 70th Seven, the Desolator is not. We have seen how the 70th Seven and the seventh trumpet align, leaving seven remaining bowls of God's most severe and complete judgment yet to be poured out.

> Then I saw another sign in heaven, great and marvelous, seven angels who had seven plagues, which are the last, because in them the wrath of God is finished. (Rev. 15:1, NASB)

This is where we pick up this next link. Once Jesus has begun to reign at the seventh trumpet, there is this remaining nasty business of subduing the enemies of God.

> And the seventh angel sounded; and there were great voices in heaven, saying, The kingdoms of this world are become the kingdoms of our Lord, and of his Christ; and he shall reign for ever and ever. (Rev. 11:15)

> We give You thanks, O Lord God, the Almighty, who are and who were, because You have taken Your great power and have begun to reign. And the nations were enraged. (Rev. 11:17-18, NASB)

The Desolator and his global empire will be the focus of the wrath of God.

> Then the fifth angel poured out his bowl on the throne of the beast, and his kingdom became darkened.... (Rev. 16:10, NASB)

Just because Jesus has begun to reign doesn't mean that those who oppose him are instantly gone. The system that was set up, "great Babylon," needs to be destroyed for all its atrocities against the Holy One.

> ...for thy merchants were the great men of the earth; for by thy sorceries were all nations deceived. And in her was found the blood of prophets, and of saints, and of all that were slain upon the earth. (Rev. 18:23-24)

> And the seventh angel poured out...and the cities of the nations fell: and great Babylon came in remembrance before God, to give unto her the cup of the wine of the fierceness of his wrath. (Rev. 16:17,19)

The system that was will no longer be. As we begin to look at the secondary passages of End-Times scripture in the following chapter, you will see that many of them flesh out this particular aspect of End-Times doctrine. The 30 days represents the period of the second global judgment that will destroy the earth, both physically and socially.

As you read through the fierce characteristics of the bowl judgments in Revelation 16, you may notice that 30 days would be the proper length of time that the earth's inhabitants and ecosystem are likely to survive, given the total scale of the devastation. The second bowl stands out as perhaps the death knell of the earth.

> And the second angel poured out his vial upon the sea; and it became as the blood of a dead man: and every living soul died in the sea. (Rev. 16:3)

When this happens, we know that the earth's ability to replenish oxygen will have been terminally disabled. Couple that with the fourth bowl, during which all the vegetation flames up due to increased heat from the sun, creating a rock of putrid seas with a suffocating atmosphere.

The enraged nations of the earth will need to do all they can to retake Jerusalem to have any hope of restoring the previous order. Under the leadership of the Desolator (the Antichrist or "beast"), their armies will rally at a plain nearby to storm the city. This is where the term "Armageddon" comes from. It describes the name of the open valley, the valley of Meggido, that the nations will use as their staging area into Jerusalem. They come to make war, but only find death.

> And I saw the beast, and the kings of the earth, and their armies, gathered together to make war against him that sat on the horse, and against his army. And the beast was taken, and with him the false prophet that wrought miracles before him, with which he deceived them that had received the mark of the beast, and them that worshipped his image. These both were cast alive into a lake of fire burning with brimstone. (Rev. 19:19-20)

This marks the first 30 days of Jesus' reign. What follows is an unprecedented reign of peace and prosperity. Daniel 12:12 tells us of the blessing that comes to those who wait the additional 45 days after God has restored the earth to a redeemed state where the lion and lamb lie down together (Isa. 65:25). This is all reminiscent of the Christian life. Just as the Holy Spirit moves into a messed-up sinner's life, so Jesus invades the fallen earth. Both of them must die to themselves and be reborn into something better. Yes, sin is still a practical reality, but both are, in a sense, "new creations" (2 Cor. 5:17).

Part III

He spoke to me: "Son of man, look with your eyes,
listen with your ears, and pay attention to everything
I am going to show you, for you have been brought
here so that I might show it to you.

(Eze 40:4—HCSB)

16

Following the Blueprint of Group 1

To this point, we have only compared primary scriptures with each other to see if we can discover whether God has placed a blueprint in the Bible for us to use in building an End-Times doctrine. We started by declaring that God's Word is coherent and He wants us to know what its message is. We then acknowledged that we all have biases and that we should seek ways of understanding the Bible that minimize input from our own imaginations.

Placing these together, we were able to recognize a method that would cut through our human "madness" of always trying to be right. We found that method by simply comparing scripture passages that were specifically on the topic of the End Times, that were clear and detailed, and that discussed order and sequence. Of all the passages in the Bible, we found only six that significantly stood above the rest. Assuming that God wants us to understand His Word, and knowing that these six scriptures represent the primary core teaching of the End-Times doctrine, we then sought to "read the blueprint."

Fortunately, as we studied these "primary" passages, we noticed that, in Matt. 24:15, Jesus gave us the very example we required in order to understand. He told us to compare the similarities in His teaching with other primary scriptures. In this particular case, Jesus pointed to the Abomination of Desolation spoken of in Daniel as a key to understanding His teaching in the Olivet Discourse. In other words, Jesus interlinked these passages and asked us (through the disciples) to understand how they complement each other. This gave us our first connection. Another way of saying it is that Jesus showed us where to set our first column to build our End-Times structure of understanding.

What did this first "column" tell us? We discovered that the source of these trials and persecutions begin at the midpoint of a seven-year period when an abomination is set up in the holiest part of the rebuilt temple. We learned that the temple would remain defiled until the end of this seven-year period, but that there would be a 30-day period afterwards related to the one who defiled it. The precise time periods given in Daniel point to the fact that the temple will be purified instantly at the end of the seven-year period when the "most Holy" is anointed.

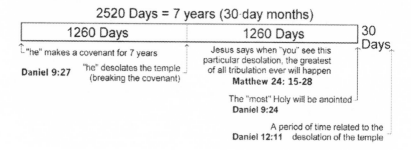

2520 Days = 7 years (30-day months)

1260 Days	1260 Days	30 Days
"he" makes a covenant for 7 years **Daniel 9:27** "he" desolates the temple (breaking the covenant)	Jesus says when "you" see this particular desolation, the greatest of all tribulation ever will happen **Matthew 24: 15-28** The "most" Holy will be anointed **Daniel 9:24** A period of time related to the **Daniel 12:11** desolation of the temple	

Jesus' first connection lays the foundation work for all else that follows. This connection identified the beginning, midpoint, and end of the 70th Seven, followed by a 30-day period, after which the Antichrist (or Desolator) is destroyed. The 30-day, post-70th Seven period allows for the "consummation" and "poured-out" decree spoken of in Dan. 9:27. We saw this addressed in our last connection regarding the bowl judgments in Revelation. These connections are systematically organized in such a fashion that we could logically come full circle to define and close the structure, just as a blueprint defines a building structure.

Having seen the overall scheme of the final "seven" in the first link, our second link was the next logical step to see if any of the other primary scriptures helped to further define the final seven. The most likely candidate is the complete panorama given to us in Revelation. Daniel 9:24 defines what will happen when the 70th Seven is complete. After examining these six promises, all of which are looking toward a literal fulfillment, we then read the book of Revelation, looking for a match. We found it at the seventh trumpet in Revelation 10:7, 11:15, 19 when it is declared that the world now belongs to Jesus.

This link further defined the structure of the 70th Seven by identifying its termination at the seventh trumpet in Revelation when Jesus begins to *literally* reign by *literally* standing on Mt. Zion as we later depicted in Revelation 14 when the core (144,000 first fruits) of Israel receives the promises God gave to Abraham.

We then jumped to another link that describes the event that leads up to the protection of this group of 144,000 men, which included the sudden arrival in heaven of people from all tribes, tongues and nations. The darkening of the sun, moon, and stars represents that link. Two of our primary passages, Matt. 24: 29–31 and Rev. 6:11–7:1, describe a series of events that comes before, during, and after this dimming of heavenly light sources. As we lined these two passages up side-by-side, we immediately saw the similarities: the tribulations beforehand, the mourning and hiding of the world from the glory of God during, and then the angels going all over the earth with people who identify with Jesus being delivered (the elect in Matt. 24:31 and those whom Jesus is comforting in Rev. 7:9–17).

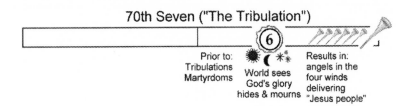

At this stage, we could be fairly confident that we could identify the sixth seal of Revelation with the Rapture. We did not know the sixth seal's exact location within the 70th Seven, but just as Jesus explained, we can learn how to recognize the season of the seals. However, before we could say for sure that the "Rapture" is to occur at the sixth seal, we had to line these passages up with two other very clear and explicit passages on this subject from 1 and 2 Thessalonians.

The next two links then led us down that path of coldly and callously comparing these passages side-by-side to see if they spoke of similar events in similar sequence. We began with lining up 1 Thess. 4:13–5:11 with Matt. 24:30–33, 38–39, and 42–43. We also noted that Paul's teaching claimed to match up and be from our Lord Jesus, further bolstering the idea that God's Word is coherent and that consequently all these primary passages on the same topic should communicate the same sequence. Once again, the parallels were obvious in the details and in the idioms and descriptions employed.

70th Seven ("The Tribulation")

Matthew 24's Description
(which includes the sun, moon, and stars event)
speaks of Jesus appearing in glory
at a UNIQUE trumpet sounding
when "Jesus people" are gathered together.
And then we can understand the seasons and
realize the world will not see it coming because
they are living life as "usual" when the Lord comes back
as a "thief in the night" to destroy them.

"RAPTURE"

1 Thessalonians 4-5 Description
The Lord appears noticeably with a
SHOUT & ANGELIC VOICE & TRUMP;
a unique trump blown by God and
"Jesus people" are caught up together.
And we of the light should know the seasons,
but the world will not because they will live
life as "usual" and be caught off guard by the
"thief in the night" who destroys them.

We then approached 2 Thessalonians 2 to see if its sequence matched that of the other passages. In his second letter, Paul clarified some misconceptions that resulted from his earlier letter, 1 Thessalonians. The sequence laid out in Matthew 24 showed us that, after a time of tribulation, Jesus would come and gather the "Jesus people" to Himself. Then, He described the destruction of the unbelieving world by making a parallel to the time of Noah. This order is repeated in 1 Thessalonians as the Lord appears with all the noticeable fanfare of the shout, voice, and trumpet, *enough to wake the dead*, then gathers the "Jesus people." This is followed by a description of how the world will be suddenly destroyed.

Finally, in comparing 2 Thessalonians 2, we saw the exact same sequence of events repeated in the first three verses, which describe the coming of the Lord, followed by the gathering together of the "Jesus people,"[46] followed by a reference to the "Day of Christ," which is another way of saying the "Day of the Lord," with special emphasis on Jesus' actions.

As the framework of our End-Times doctrine was going up piece by piece, we were also beginning to witness how other parts naturally began fitting together. This term, "Day of Christ," connected us to another unique term in Revelation at the sixth seal, "wrath of the Lamb." Both are related to the time when God signals to the world that the Day of the Lord has arrived and He is going to begin His wrath. The sign given throughout the Old Testament is the darkening of the sun, moon, and stars.

It became evident that these four passages, Revelation 6, Matthew 24, 1 Thessalonians 4–5, and 2 Thessalonians 2, were all lining up and that the sequence that they share—Jesus' arrival, the Rapture, followed by God's wrath—all were to occur after the man of lawlessness appears to defile the temple, as 2 Thess. 2:3 so specifically states.

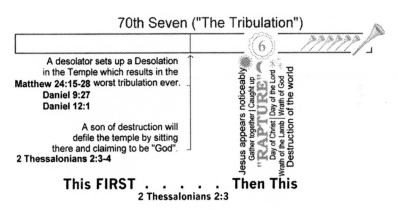

70th Seven ("The Tribulation")

A desolator sets up a Desolation in the Temple which results in the **Matthew 24:15-28** worst tribulation ever. **Daniel 9:27** **Daniel 12:1**

A son of destruction will defile the temple by sitting there and claiming to be "God". **2 Thessalonians 2:3-4**

Jesus appears noticeably / Gather together / Caught up / "RAPTURE" / Day of Christ / Day of the Lord / Wrath of the Lamb / Wrath of God / Destruction of the world

This FIRST . . . . . Then This
2 Thessalonians 2:3

---

[46] "Jesus people" is a term I use to simply describe "people who identify with Jesus." Some people get hung up on the differences between "elect" and "saints," when in reality, Jesus is gathering His people (the elect) in Matthew 24 and is comforting His people in Revelation 7. In both cases, these people identify with Jesus.

Having confirmed the position of the sixth seal within the second half of the 70th Seven, we then sought to place the other seals within the final seven by looking at Jesus' description of the events leading up to His arrival and the Rapture of the church. As we compared Matt. 24:5–39 with the seals of Revelation, we immediately recognized the stark parallels. This continued to define our overall understanding of the sequence and order of the End Times by showing us that the 70th Seven begins with the first seal, reaches its midpoint somewhere between the third and fourth seals, where we surmise that the "Desolator" of the temple begins global persecutions.

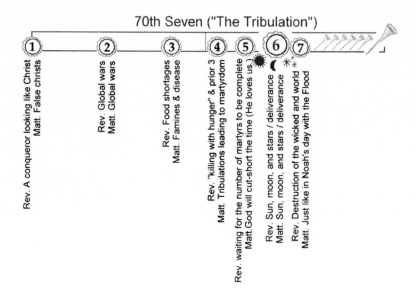

We then sought to understand the "birth pang" analogy given by both Jesus and Paul in relation to these events, which continued to confirm the spacing and order of the seals as they related to "you," the Christian recipient of the disciples' teachings (Matt. 28:19–20). Things would begin slowly at the beginning with a "christ-like" figure upholding a seven-year treaty with Israel, with that figure then gaining power to the point where he can "have his way" 3 1/2 years later.

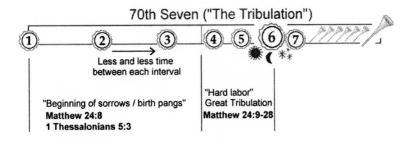

We then noticed that this period of "labor" is an unknown time of duration. This led us to see that many times of unknown duration were spoken of in relation to the same period of time from our primary scriptures. We were, therefore, able to see that these unknown durations of time were all occurring within a segment of a previously mentioned *known* duration of time: the second half of the 70th Seven (see chart below). This period of time was established as 1260 days, 42 months, and "a time, times and half a time" in various locations within our primary passages.

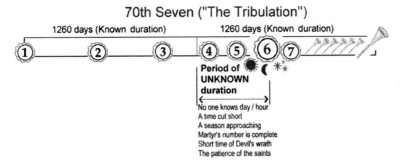

Finally, as we sought to complete our overall picture of the grand timeline given in the Revelation of Jesus Christ, the last book of the Bible, we took a look at the bowl judgments and their purpose in timing and location and the necessity for their dispensing to be brief.

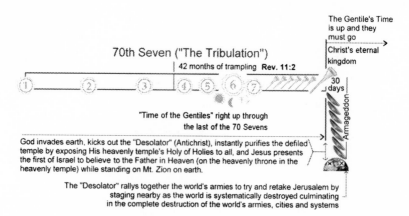

This last structural beam allowed us to complete our view and doctrine of the End Times, returning us to focus on the extra 30 days resonating from the abomination at the midpoint of the last seven that we studied in the first link.

When we look at this structure as a whole—as an End-Times doctrine—no other scriptures change this understanding, for no other scriptures approach the clarity in detail or sequence, or match the topical nature of these six or seven we discovered previously. Placed together, these scriptures build a solid doctrine using Jesus' example of reading the blueprints. The structure established looks like this:

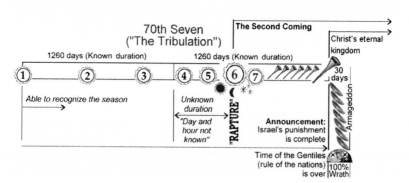

In the next section, we will look at the secondary scriptures and see how they enhance our current understanding.

17

Placing Secondary Components of Group 2

> "What's holding that up?" my boss asked me. "Skyhooks?"
>
> I looked back down at the large trellis on the architectural drawing as he continued. "Shouldn't there be posts to hold that thing up?"
>
> I had gotten so caught up in my design that I had completely forgotten about the support structure, leaving it up to those magical hooks in the sky.
>
> I learned a valuable lesson that day. Don't come up with grand building elements unless you have a way to support them.

Earlier, we divided the End-Times scriptures into three groups: the primary passages, the secondary passages, and the related, but less specific passages that give us hints. In this chapter, we'll discuss the secondary passages—those that need structure to be held up in place.

Though these scriptures are beautiful in and of themselves, they make better End-Times sense when placed within the context of the clearer and more detailed passages on the same topic. These secondary scriptures are analogous to building components that fit within an existing structure. They must be interpreted in light of the clearer. Lest you think we would have to force that interpretation, think again. Interpreting these less clear passages in the light of the more clear passages should be a natural fit, given the simple alignments of the primary scriptures.

Group 2: The In-Between

Psalm 18:1–20	Isaiah 64:1–5	Matthew 13:37–43
Psalm 110	Ezekiel 37–39	Matthew 25
Isaiah 2:10–22	Daniel 2:19–45, 3	Luke 17:22–36
Isaiah 13:9–13	Daniel 7	Luke 21:5–38
Isaiah 24	Daniel 8	Romans 11:25–26
Isaiah 26:19–27:1	Joel	1 Corinthians 15:20–56
Isaiah 28:15–22	Zechariah 12-14	2 Peter 2:4–9, 3:3–13

Another reason the secondary passages must be interpreted in light of the primary passages is to avoid ending up with "the tail wagging the dog." Adhering to these basics of biblical interpretation will prevent the type of inverted scholarship that satisfies personal biases.

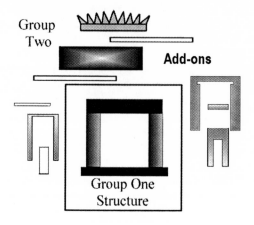

This is not to say that some of these passages do not contain a sequence of sorts. They do. However, they are not specifically discussing or teaching the order and sequence of End-Times events. These middle category passages are devoted to communicating another aspect of God's deliverance, and any reference to order and sequence is used only in support of the main point of the passage.

This is a critical difference between primary and secondary passages. Where primary passages come out and plainly reveal the order and sequence of End-Times events, secondary passages mention some of these events in support of another point or even a different topic entirely. Some of these passages are specific to the

End Times and others are not. It will become apparent as you study these passages that none of them comes close to the clarity or specificity of the primary passages, even though they are much more specific than those listed in Group 3. We will briefly address some of these passages just enough for you to see whether they fit naturally within the framed doctrine set by the clearest and most detailed scriptures. These passages help qualify our understanding of a few related items that are integral to the End Times that I will further explain as appropriate.

Unlike the discussion of the Group 1 passages, I will not attempt to show these correlations by placing the scriptures side by side. Because of the number of scriptures, and the length of these passages, this would be impractical. Instead, I will ask you, the reader, to read these scriptures on your own and look up the correlations for yourself.

The Secondary Passages

Psalm 18:1–20 is about the rightful ruler, David, fleeing from Saul. It is a repeat of 2 Sam. 22:1–21. There are some wonderful alignments here with David and the saints, Saul and the Antichrist, and the last few seals. Let's look at a few.

First, King Saul knew his days were numbered, just as the Antichrist and the Devil know their days are numbered (Rev. 12:12). King Saul was enraged by the fact that there was a new king (kingdom) to take over, just as the nations led by the Antichrist will be enraged that they will no longer rule (Rev. 12:10–12, 11:17–18). King Saul hunted and persecuted David, just the Antichrist will hunt and persecute the saints (Rev. 13:7)—or as Jesus says, "you" will be hunted and persecuted after the abomination (Matt. 24:9–28). David was the future ruler, just as the saints are future rulers (Rev. 5:10, 1:6). David fled, and Jesus said to flee (Matt. 24:15–16).

Furthermore, we see "sorrows of death" in verse 4 and "sorrows of Hades" in verse 5 that correspond with the time of persecution of the saints at the fourth and fifth seals, when they must choose between physical death resulting in martyrdom or spiritual death resulting from prolonging physical life in the Antichrist's system by wearing his "mark" (Revelation 13). Also, when God finally moves to deliver David, David records that God hears from His temple in heaven (verse 6); compare this to the sixth seal in Revelation where we see God on His throne in His temple in heaven when He removes the saints from the Great Tribulation. Then the earth and hills shake in verse 7, just as the mountains shake at the sixth seal. As the heavens bow in verse 9, resulting in God appearing, so do the heavens roll-up like a scroll ("split apart," NASB) at the sixth seal. Just as David is "drawn up" by God out of the waters in verses 16–19, so will the saints be "caught up" out of the nations from an enemy too strong for them (Psalm 18:17, Rev. 13:7).

It should be clear that the purpose of Psalm 18 is the topic and not the sequence. In fact, it remained in the Group 3 for quite awhile until these parallels became very apparent, at which point I then decided to bump it up to Group 2. Therefore, it is one of the weaker ones of the second group.

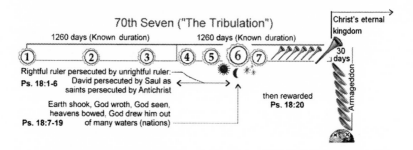

Psalm 110 is frequently quoted by New Testament writers and speaks to the time in which the Messiah is ruling from Zion and will destroy His enemies. It finds alignment with our understanding of Christ reigning at the end of the 70th Seven in the midst of His enemies, with 30 days allotted for the bowls before Armageddon. Verse two aligns with the Rev. 11:18 when the nations were enraged because Jesus had begun to rule.

> The LORD shall send the rod of thy strength out of Zion:
> rule thou in the midst of thine enemies. (Psalm 110:2)

In Rev. 14:1–5, we see Jesus (the Lamb) standing on Zion and yet also before the throne, suggesting that the heavenly temple has physically manifested itself on earth. It is during this time that the enemies of Christ continue for an additional 30 days before their final destruction.

> The Lord at thy right hand shall strike through kings in the day of his wrath. (Psalm 110:5)

Jesus will be ruling in the midst of his enemies for 30 days until He treads the winepress of the wrath of God and destroys the nations. This all aligns with what we've learned about Armageddon and the desire of the nations to make their final attempt to regain control of the world by destroying the physically manifested Kingdom of God in Jerusalem. The "Time of the Gentiles" is up, and they must be destroyed now that this authority has been granted.

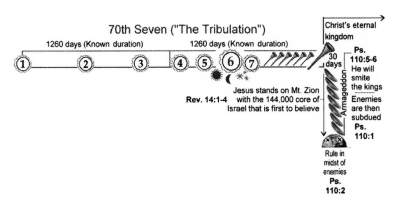

Isaiah 2:10–22 provides us with direct associations with the hiding of men in the rocks when they see God's glory. It is no stretch to see how the sixth seal also shows men hiding from God's glory. In other words, by comparing men's reactions, we see that Jesus is appearing gloriously at the time when saints are "Raptured up" and the wrath of God is ready to begin.

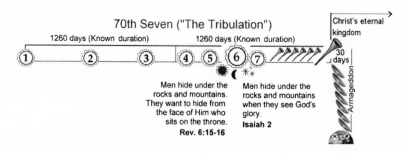

Isaiah 13:9–13 could easily be expanded to include most of the chapter. This passage ties in with the sixth seal at the signs of the sun, moon, and stars in verse 10. At the 6th Seal, God begins to act by rescuing the righteous and initiating His wrath against the wicked world. In Isaiah 13, God says that He will punish the world for its evil in verse 11. The two passages begin to tie the world of man to "Babylon, glory of the kingdoms" (Isa. 13:19). There is a good reason to see the world of man as "great Babylon," particularly in light of Rev. 16:19; when God remembers Babylon, all the cities of the nations fall..

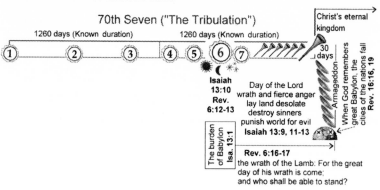

Isaiah 24 continues to build on the idea that the world of man is "great Babylon." The alignments here with Revelation 17–18 are astounding. For instance, the seven-fold fall of the earth in verses 18–20 is very similar to the utter fall of Babylon; neither shall rise again. The descriptions in these passages of lost joy and gaiety are similar. Even more compelling is the parallel between Isaiah 24:10's reference to the "city of chaos" and the references in Rev. 17:18, 18:10,16, 18, 19, 21 to great Babylon as a city.

Permit me this diversion to explain. It is no mistake that Revelation uses the term "great Babylon" to describe the nations of the End Times. The roots of this "great Babylon" extend past the ancient empire of Babylon right back to the first city of man in the post-Flood era. Genesis 11 recounts for us the story of the Tower of Babel, where the majority of mankind decided that they would determine their own destiny by unifying against God's command. As a result, God confounded their languages so that they dispersed across the globe, segregating into distinct people groups with shared characteristics over time. It is only a matter of time before mankind overcomes the barriers that God inflicted. Mankind will one day be a "great Babylon." It is this confusion of languages at Babel, "the city of chaos," then the reunification of man during what we call the "End Times," that taken together, define this age of mankind like bookends.

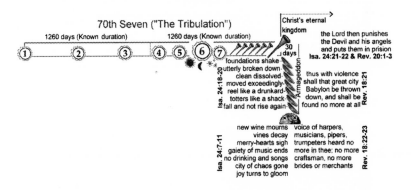

Isaiah 26:19–27:1 continues to be relevant to our search for truth. It speaks of the same sequence that we have understood in the seals of Revelation. There is a resurrection and then, for Israel, a sealing of 144,000 who are to be preserved to physically receive the promises of God at the end of the 70 sets of seven. These 144,000 are protected from God's wrath as He punishes the world that has attempted to hide what it has done (Isa. 26:21). Again, we can find parallels here with Rev. 18:24, where "great Babylon," the harlot system, was responsible for the spilled blood of the saints. Then the next verse, Isaiah 27:1, says that God will punish the "dragon" (the Devil and his system) at this time, as well. This

113

also finds an interesting parallel with the harlot riding a beast in Rev. 17:2–8, empowered by the "dragon" in Rev. 13:1–2.

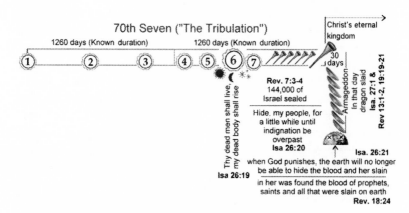

Isaiah 28:15–22 gives us further illumination as to the nature of the confirmed seven-year covenant mentioned in Dan. 9:27. God calls this a "covenant with death" (vv. 15, 18) and "with hell we are at agreement" (vv. 15, 18). Now I think we have seen these two fellows, Death and Hell, referenced elsewhere. They are the enforcers of something during the fourth seal, and Jesus holds the power over them by having their "keys" (Rev. 1:18). How did (or, shall I say, *will*) Israel get into this fix of making a deal with the Devil? Verse 16 is quick to explain. Israel has built its current national identity on a wrong foundation. The people did not use the precious cornerstone of Jesus to determine all that should follow thereafter. In ancient architecture, a cornerstone determined the precise corner, and all the rest of the structure followed based upon its placement. It was the most important part of the structure. Since they missed Jesus, they missed the overall purpose and destiny for their nation during the Time of the Gentiles.

We are seeing the contrast between the Christ and the Antichrist being alluded to here, as well. Whereas the "covenant with death" is full of lies and falsehood, the cornerstone covenant with Christ is faithful and true (Isaiah 26:15–16). One covenant will be brokered as part of the global deception, while the other has already been paid for and is waiting to be established. It does seem as if Israel will once again place its hope nationally in man rather than the Creator of man. Israel's right to exist does not depend upon men and their treaties.

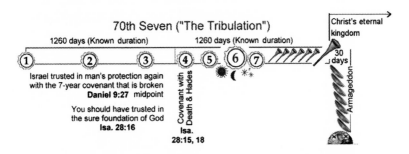

Isaiah 64:1–5 illuminates our understanding of the sixth seal as referring to the Rapture and the beginning of God's wrath.

> Oh that thou wouldest rend the heavens, that thou wouldest come down, that the mountains might flow down at thy presence. (Isa. 64:1)

Verse 1 highlights a number of things we have seen recorded at the sixth seal: rending the heavens, mountains falling down, and God's presence.

Like Isaiah 2, this passage explains that God comes out of heaven during this time. When God comes out for wrath, He also comes out to meet His righteous (Isaiah 64:5) so that they can be with him to experience what the eye has not seen nor the mind perceived (Isa. 64:4). Jesus said He goes to heaven to prepare a place for us, and He will return for us (John 14:2–3). In Isa. 64:4–5, God has also prepared something for His righteous.

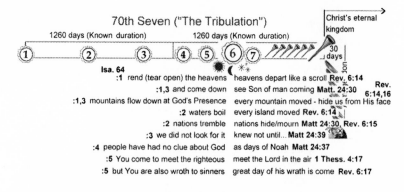

Ezekiel 37–39 has its focus on the fulfillment of God's promises to Israel by defeating her enemies and restoring the nation's relationship with God. At a surface level, I see good reason to connect the battle mentioned here with that of Armageddon, particularly in light of certain similarities to other clear Armageddon verses. In Eze. 38:2, there is a leader, Gog, who is in charge of three other entities. This is very similar to other references in Daniel 7 regarding the final leader who uproots three other kings. Then there is the call to the birds to come and feast on the kings in Eze. 39:17–20, which is very similar to what happens at Armageddon in Rev. 19:17–18, 21. And finally, in Eze. 39:22, we see God placing His glory before the nations just before He destroys them. In comparing this with Psalm 110, it again shows that Jesus will reign and then destroy the nations, which no longer are allowed to have control.

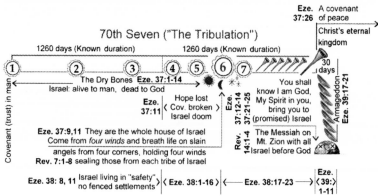

Daniel 2:19–45 and 3 provide us with another glimpse of mankind's empires as man-made idols that will be utterly destroyed and forever replaced by a non-man-made empire, God's kingdom. These chapters continue to identify "great Babylon" as a type of man's global society during the End Times. The identical phrase and attitude is used in Dan. 4:30 so that the infestation in the "head of gold"[47] characterizes all that follows. Notice that the statue is an idol, carefully crafted by the hands of a man, while the stone of God's eternal empire is cut from the mountain without hands. God's eternal kingdom is of a completely different nature; one not metallic and shiny like precious metals or swords.

After hearing the interpretation of this dream from Daniel, the king's pride swelled to the point that he thought he must be the kingdom, head to foot. Thus, he built a 60-cubit-high statue that represented the fullness of measure. The ancient Babylonian math system had a base 60 as opposed to our base 10 today. By making the statue "60" high, he was also saying that he is the end all of being—Mr. Complete, himself.

I find it interesting that as we find evidence mounting that points to the End Times world as being "great Babylon," our current modern world is measured by systems that are Babylonian. We measure time and space according to standards set by the Babylonians; each minute is 60 seconds, each hour is 60 minutes,

---

[47] What if the face of the "head of gold" was, in fact, that of Nebuchadnezzar himself? This might explain his extreme behavior towards the wise men of Babylon. All kings had dreams, and for that reason, wise men had books of dream interpretation. Nebuchadnezzar would have been aware of this, since he grew up the son of a king and had probably heard a number of canned interpretations given by the wise men over the years. But when Nebuchadnezzar saw the statue of "himself" destroyed, he wanted more. He wanted a response he could trust. To his great relief, Daniel was able to provide that response, and the king realized he was just the head of gold. The vision, though given to the king, was also a message to the Jews. For it started to make sense of their loss of the Promised Land and their captivity by revealing that God is in charge of the nations and their progression. The Jews were promised a land, but then an evil empire that worshipped a foreign god came and took them over. Habakkuk 1 records the chagrin of that prophet upon learning the shocking truth. In Daniel 2, God explained that some day, His kingdom would, indeed, reign supreme.

a circle is made up of 360 degrees[48] or six units of 60. Our world is mapped and surveyed by this system of degrees, minutes, and seconds. As an architect, when I draw a site plan, I follow the surveyor's measurements that are recorded in the following format: North x-degrees, y-minutes, z-seconds East.

The progression of kingdoms through time points to a gap at the statue's ankle, where the description turns to the mottled and non-cohesive nature of the feet and toes. God's kingdom has yet to utterly destroy these historical nations represented by the different metals of the statue. This destruction did not occur at Jesus' First Coming, because the Church was started before Rome's peak of power. The Church never literally destroyed the statue and the systems it represented. No other empire really took over Rome; it just slowly fragmented into the nations of Europe and the Middle East. In 476 A.D., Rome—the capital of the Western leg of the empire—fell to the Europeans, who later adopted Roman systems.

Just as the nations of the statue were literal, so will be their literal destruction at the hands of Jesus at His Second Coming. The final empire will spring from the territory occupied by the ancient Roman Empire.

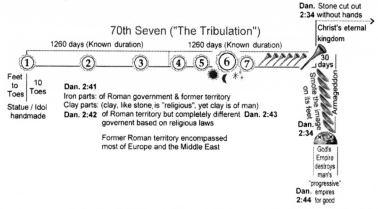

[48] Sixes are units of measure given to men because God created man on the sixth day. He perpetuated that in the cycles of seasons. The reckoning of time during the beginning of the global Flood equates five months with 150 days (compare Gen. 7:24, 8:3 with 7:11, 8:4). This implies that a yearly cycle was indeed 360 days. This would explain why a circle has traditionally been segmented into 360 degrees.

Daniel 7 continues the theme of the succeeding empires from where Daniel 2 left off, but this time, it relays them as beasts rather than parts of an idol. In this passage, we get one of our first glimpses of the Antichrist as seen in the boasting horn, who is also a king who wears the saints down. The characteristics align with similar accounts in Dan. 11:16, Dan. 21:7, 2 Thess. 2:4, and Revelation 13, where the saints are being hunted and persecuted.

This passage narrowly missed making it into the select group of passages that defined the End-Times doctrine. It meets most of the criteria set forth earlier except it is just a little less clear, I felt, than the others. Although, even if it were added, it is apparent that the events portrayed clearly align with all that has already been established.

In comparing the secondary passages we've seen thus far, we could surmise that that a covenant will be made in good faith with Israel and 10 nations of Roman territorial origin. Three of these nations will be overtaken by one new power at the midpoint when the covenant is broken. This new configuration will seek to persecute the saints (Dan. 7:21); then, in verse 9, authority is taken away from the final empire by God. The "horn" continues on after he has lost authority in verse 11, only to meet his doom. We know that the Desolator will continue on for 30 days after the desolation is removed, only to be destroyed at Armageddon and cast into the Lake of Fire (Dan. 7:11, Rev. 19:20). Furthermore, Dan. 7:8–14 solidifies the alignment of the seventh trumpet of Revelation with the end of the 70th Seven by showing us one more time that the end of the beast's dominion equates with the beginning of the "son of man's" dominion.

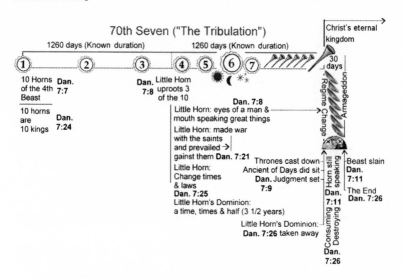

Daniel 8 purports itself to be somewhat of a sequel to the vision of Chapter 7; however, it focuses on the second and third empires of Chapter 7 and also looks at the "little horn" as coming from one of the four offspring horns of the third empire rather than a new uprooting horn of the fourth empire.[49] Here we see the working of the scriptural principle of "foreshadowing then ultimate fulfillment." Just as there was a precursor to the Antichrist in the form of Antiochus Epiphanes before the First

---

[49] Daniel 5:30-31 shows Medo-Persia taking over Babylon, making Medo-Persia the second empire of silver in Daniel 2 and the bear leaning on its side in Daniel 7. Daniel 8 defines the two empires of the ram and goat as Persia and Greece. Therefore, we know that Greece is the third empire of bronze in Daniel 2 and the four-headed, four-winged leopard of Daniel 7. Daniel 10:20 and 11:2 also report the same sequence. The fourth empire of iron legs in Daniel 2 and the strong beast with iron teeth in Daniel 7 are never identified, but we do know that the third and fourth empires are different and that the metal greater than bronze is iron. Therefore, when the "little horn" arises from Greece in Chapter 8, it must be a foreshadow or type of the future and ultimate reality that arises out of the empire that will take over Greece. From history, we know that Rome took over Greece, just as Greece took over Persia, and Persia took over Babylon. This literal string of events demands a literal fulfillment in the same sense: God's literal, physical kingdom on earth after having taken over the previous kingdoms.

Coming of Christ, so will there be an ultimate fulfillment of the Antichrist before the Second Coming of Christ.

> He said, "Behold, I will make known to you what shall be at the latter end of the indignation, for it refers to the appointed time of the end. (Daniel 8:19, ESV)

Verse 19 begins the transition from 168 B.C. to the End Times by stating that what Daniel has just seen up to this point will have both a "near" and "far" fulfillment. It will both happen in the near future, but it also awaits a longer-term, ultimate fulfillment. Verse 22 completes the transition from the first "antichrist" to the End-Times Antichrist, placing the 2,300 evenings and mornings in verse 14 squarely in the past contextually. There are two plain and simple reasons this means what it says: 2300 days. First, this is referring to the removal of the evening and morning sacrifices. The temple was defiled and the prescribed sacrifices for each evening and morning in Exodus 29:39 could no longer be carried out. Second, in Genesis 1, the evenings and mornings associated with numbers are plainly meant to be understood as 24-hour days. If God wanted to leave the term open to the idea of "days equals years," He would have used the Hebrew word for "day" rather than spelling out the two things that define a literal day, the setting and rising of the sun. Here, we see the same pattern of "evenings" and "mornings" associated with numbers, so, once again, we know that they are meant to be understood as 24-hour days.

It is this potential confusion and the specific focus on only the second and third empires that caused me to locate this passage in the second group, even though it does refer to an Abomination of Desolation that Jesus points to in Matt. 24:15. This passage is just not as clear and specific as the others.

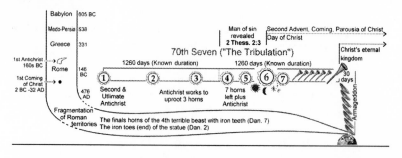

The book of Joel is on the topic of the Day of the Lord, as is stated three times (Joel 1:15, 2:1, 3:1). The signs of the start of the Day of the Lord are mentioned no less than three times (Joel 2:10, 2:31, 3:15) throughout the book. For this reason, it is difficult, at best, to be sure about any order of events. Instead, we should focus on the writer's main message: repent before it is too late. This is a prime example of how we should interpret a less clear passage in light of a more cohesive body of clear passages. In the book, we find elements that are part of our already established timeline and, when placed appropriately, make perfect sense to our "Greek" way of linear thinking. However, as is often the case in getting out a life-and-death warning, avoiding the pitfall is the main point. Sequences are subordinate.

For instance, in Joel 2:31–32 we see the signs of the Day of the Lord and then (a little or a lot) of time elapses to show that there will be deliverance and escape on Mt. Zion. If we look to our current understanding, we see that there is a group of 144,000 Israelites sealed for protection from God's wrath at the sixth seal; then, they appear on Mt. Zion with Jesus (now their Deliverer and Savior) to be presented to God in a restored relationship at the seventh trumpet. So in this case, the time elapse between verses 31–32 is through the seven trumpets of Revelation, which likely takes at least a year.

Joel 3 introduces a new element, just as we would expect in a Second Group text. The element is not critical to the sequence and order of events, but it helps define something we have already established regarding the Rapture as the first event of the Second Coming. This element involves the valley and hill that lay immediately east of and between Mt. Zion and the Mount of Olives. Joel uses the term "the valley of Jehoshaphat" rather than the current name, the Kidron Valley. The name change highlights

God's judgment in Joel 3:2, because "Jehoshaphat" means "Jehovah's judgment." It points back to the time in Israel's history when God gave them victory over a coalition of seemingly united enemies (2 Chr. 20:20–26, Ps. 83:6–8). This federation of nations connects to the times when Jerusalem will be trampled by the nations (Rev. 11:2) and the 10 toes and 10 horns in Daniel 2 and 7 to name a few. It is during this time that Jesus returns begins His Wrath. This valley is not to be confused with the valley of Armageddon, which is located in a different geography to the north and will be used by a coalition or federation of all nations as a military staging ground to try to regain Jerusalem at the end of the 30-day period following the 70th Seven.

One cannot speak of the Kidron Valley without speaking of the hills framing the valley. The Mount of Olives is the hill directly east of Mt. Zion. Mark 13:3 describes Jesus sitting on the Mount of Olives so that He could see the temple. Mark's account provides a reference point for Jesus' Olivet Discourse describing the events surrounding His return. When Jesus returns, the believers who have already died are resurrected bodily from death. Today, the Kidron Valley and base of the Mount of Olives is a massive graveyard. When placed within our existing timeline, we can begin to understand what is happening and perhaps know where many of the disciples may actually be buried.

Consider the following: At the sixth seal, the nations see the wrath of the Lamb. This means that God has decided to judge the nations. Also, the events of the sixth seal begin only after God has determined when the number of martyrs is complete (Rev. 6:10–11). Related to this is what the two angels told the disciples (all of whom were future martyrs, except John[50]) that, when Jesus ascended to heaven from the Mount of Olives, "in like manner, you will see him come back" (Acts 1:11). At face value, one could understand the angels' words to mean that when Jesus returns, He will return to the very place from which He departed.

---

[50] Besides the betrayer, Judah, all the disciples went on to be martyrs. Although John was not a physical martyr, he was one at heart because he had the courage to show his face at the cross and risk it all for the Lord. The others were ashamed and fled. Perhaps John 21 provides a future "typology" where one of 12 will survive to see the Rapture.

All this is to say that the Day of the Lord begins here, on the Mount of Olives, from whence He left. This is the "kick-off point" for God's wrath, perhaps even the location of the last martyr and the likely burial location of many of the first martyrs. The Second Coming begins here at act one, the Rapture of the dead and living[51] and the protection of the 144,000 sealed Israelites. If the author were one of the Twelve, he would be buried on the Mount of Olives so that when he rose, he would see his Lord arrive just as He departed.[52]

In light of our sequence determined by the primary scriptures, it makes sense for Jesus to arrive first here. Besides being the place where He spent much time with the disciples (Luke 21:37–38), it also signifies that He is ready to ascend the throne. His Second Coming is made up of many acts and deeds, just as at His First Coming. He has yet to receive authority to stand on Mt. Zion. His arrival and judgment as King of kings will be announced. As the judgment is announced in the form of the seven trumpets given to us in Revelation,[53] the final pronouncement is made and the dominions change hands. Jesus then brings His

---

[51] How can the church meet the Lord in the air and be with Him forever at the Rapture when He also touches down on the Mount of Olives (Acts 1:11, Zech. 14:4)? Are these mutually exclusive or not? I don't think we can put the Lord in a box. Just as the Lord can hear my prayer with a million others and comfort me in my time of need, while also doing the same on the other side of the globe, so we can be with Him forever even though He is standing on the Mount of Olives, Mt. Zion, or anywhere else. Besides, being with Jesus forever is a state: we now have physical access to our Redeemer, whereas before (after Acts 1:11), we did not. Where can we go or flee from His presence? (Psalm 139). After the Rapture, believers will be in heaven. We can still be with the Lord after meeting with Him in the air, even if He is standing on the Mount of Olives or Mt. Zion. Please note that this interpretation is an example of letting the Scriptures lead you to an understanding rather than imposing your understanding on the Scriptures.

[52] Of course, a Christian can be buried anywhere and in any state and still be resurrected. God knows how to resurrect those eaten by lions or burned to a crisp.

[53] Trumpets are commonly associated with a call to arms; see Neh. 4:20 and Zeph. 1:14-16.

144,000 to Mt. Zion to present them to God, reconciled, redeemed, and ready to receive the Promised Land.

From Mt. Zion, during those 30 days afterwards, the Lord completes total judgment on the nations. As Joel says in 3:16, "the Lord roars out of Mt. Zion."

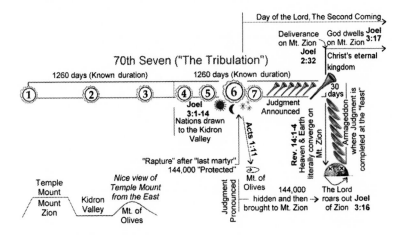

Zechariah is another book that shares all kinds of similar imagery with Revelation. The later chapters are of interest to us as they continue to reinforce the understanding of God reigning in Zion before Armageddon (Zech. 12:4–9). In Zech. 12:3, I find it interesting that Jerusalem is described as a stone that is burdensome enough to destroy the nations. In Daniel 2, the imagery of the stone "cut without hands" that crushes the empires of the statue is an amazing similarity.

Also, Zechariah 14 continues to enhance our understanding of the role of the Mount of Olives and the valley before it. If we take things at a literal face value, it appears as if the 144,000 sealed Israelites will have a chance to flee into the hidden wilderness called Azel after the graves have been burst open to let out the dead at the Rapture.

Our understanding of the Second Coming continues to expand. The Rapture is simply part of the first act. Revelation 7 describes 144,000 Israeli "firstfruit believers" being sealed and protected while the Rapture is occurring.[54] Just as our Messiah's First Coming encompassed many acts and deeds, so will His Second Coming. The presentation of the 144,000 to God on Mt. Zion is another act, while Armageddon is yet another one, too.

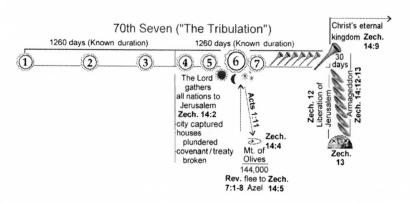

Matthew 13:37–50 is another passage that discusses angels gathering together people. Is it the Rapture or the time at the end many call the Great White Throne Judgment, just before the creation of the new heavens and new earth? Those who believe in a literal Millennium, according to Revelation 20, see the potential for another "harvest" at the end of that 1000-year period when the universe is no more and all that remains is judgment. In this scheme, there appear to be three distinct global judgments: the first was Noah's flood; the second will be events that this book has focused on, primarily up to Armageddon; and the third will be God's complete holiness revealed, resulting in the end of the earth and the fallen universe as we know it. When there is nothing left, except the Creator and His created, the final court will begin looking at all the converging factors that only God would know. Those who are not in the Book of Life are cast into the Lake of Fire. Only after all wickedness, sin, and death are cast away will

---

[54] It is possible that these 144,000 will be among others standing in the Kidron Valley and told to bow to the "image of the beast" placed above them at the temple on Mt. Zion. However, like the Daniel 3 precursor, they will resist, holding obedience to God more valuable than life. Before they are killed, the first act of the Second Coming occurs, and a way of escape is made for them through the Mount of Olives.

God produce the new heavens and new earth for the righteous to dwell in. In looking for commonalities between Matt. 13:37–50 and other passages in the Bible, the similarities with this final judgment appear to more closely align than those of the Rapture and the "Tribulation," or 70th Seven.

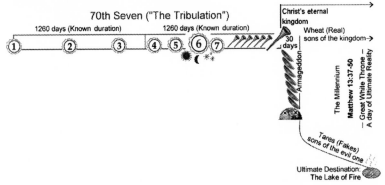

Matthew 25 is a continuation of the Olivet Discourse of Matthew 24, and provides us with three parables that further the idea that there is a group of people who take God's Word lightly and do not act upon it and end up judged, while there is another group of people who obey and are prepared and are rewarded. The final parable takes the deeds of one's life and extrapolates them to their eternal destiny.[55]

---

[55] Think of the parable of the sheep and goats in terms of sharing the gospel and "clothing in truth" during the 70th Seven, given the context of Matthew 24.

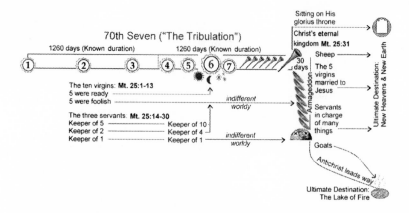

Luke 17:22–36 expands upon the points that Jesus was making towards the end of Matthew 24 and the parables in Matthew 25. We are not to be like Lot's wife, who longed for her lost world, lest we end up part of the wreckage. Revelation 18:4 admonishes the saints to "come out of" the great Babylonian harlot that we have seen represents the world and its fallen systems.

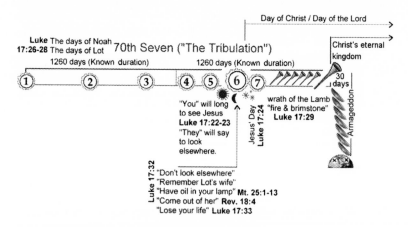

Luke 21 almost made the first group, but did not for a number of reasons. Perhaps one of the most important is that it did not set out to deal with the End-Times topic as specifically as Matthew 24 and Mark 13. Luke 21's record of what Jesus said publicly in the temple clearly contains portions that are focused on the near future of 70 A.D., while Matthew 24's and Mark 13's private explanations to the disciples focus on the End Times. (See Appendix C.)

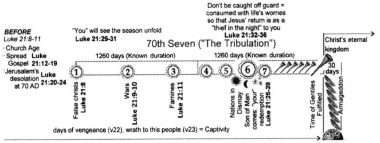

Romans 11:25–26 is a great passage to follow after discussing Luke 21, for it also discusses the Time of the Gentiles and the reason for it. In the context of Dan. 9:24–27, we can see how God has decided to reconcile all nations to Himself after the Messiah was cut off the "olive tree" by its own branches. Since then, God has been grafting the wild olive branches into the cultivated tree; and consequently, all nations and tribes and languages will be represented there some day. Eventually, this "grafting in" of the Gentile nations will end and the 144,000 first fruits from all the tribes of Israel will finally be reconciled to God. Their hearts will begin to soften when they realize that Israel utterly failed again by trusting in man rather than God. This core 144,000 will be protected and then presented to God at the end of the 70 sevens. (See Appendix B.)

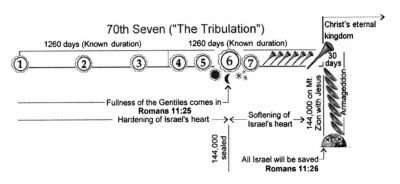

1 Corinthians 15:20–56 deals with the resurrection, its nature, and how, at the end, there will be a special group of people who will bypass death altogether and become instantly glorified. The "last trump" is comparable to the "trump of God" in 1 Thess. 4:16 and was likely understood by the Greek recipients to refer to Zech. 9:14, when God blew the trumpet to fight off a beastly Greek ruler, Antiochus Epiphanes, who foreshadows the future Antichrist by oppressing Israel and putting an abomination of desolation in the temple. The Greeks would have known their own recent history as it was played out in 168 B.C., and therefore would have understood the connection to the foreshadowed Antichrist and God's blowing of the trumpet to turn the tides and fight back once the time was ripe.

To say, as some suggest, that the "last trump" is the seventh trumpet of Revelation is misguided. John had not yet received the Revelation, so his book would not be available for almost half a century. Also, in this context, the term "last trump" is more likely to be understood as the "last call," which is more akin to what Paul said about the voice of an archangel, the shout, and the blast of a trumpet in 1 Thessalonians. When I think of this passage, I think of that hymn, "When the roll is called up yonder I'll be there…"

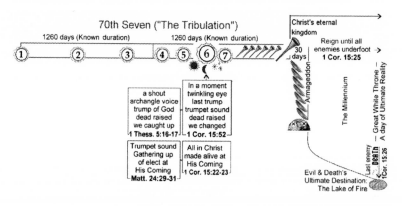

2 Peter 2:4–9, 3:3–13. Peter, like Paul, is simply relating what Jesus taught the disciples. Both Paul and Peter use the phrase "a thief coming in the night" (2 Pet. 3:10) to describe the Second Coming. God knows how to deliver the righteous and condemn the world, as the thief analogy suggests. This world is passing away, and we are not to get caught up in it.

The sixth bowl of Revelation speaks to this very fact by connecting the thief analogy to the sudden destruction of "great Babylon" via the drying up of the "great river Euphrates" at the hands of King Cyrus, whom God appoints as a type of Christ in Isa. 44:28–45:1. Revelation 18:4 tells us to come out of the system so that we are not partakers in its destruction. In other words, we are to be in the world, but not of it.

It's easy to see how some of these passages blur the lines between events when the point they are addressing is other than that of specific End-Times sequence. For example, the point of the 2 Peter passages is to encourage godly living in light of the eternal perspective because none of the material things we hold precious will last. With that license, Peter knows that the end will come in fire, but he does not know that the fire will be separated by the Millennium.[56] Decades later, John was more specific about the fiery end. He wrote that the earth will be judged by God's holy fire from His altar beginning at the trumpet blasts in Revelation 8. This judgment would continue through the bowls in Revelation 16, then be followed one thousand years later by fire from the sky when God exposes His complete holiness. At that time, the "old wine skin" Jesus spoke of in Matt. 9:17—that which we call "the universe"—bursts asunder and flees before His presence (Rev. 20:9–11). God's holy presence is the final fire that purifies and, in the process, dissolves the fallen universe.

---

[56] This is similar to how Daniel may have understood the difference between the 69th and 70th Sevens.

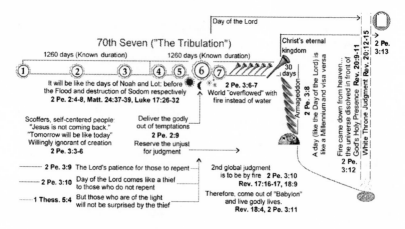

Putting It Together

How do these 20 or so passages contribute to our understanding of the End Times? None of these understandings changes the order and sequence. Rather, knowing the order and sequence from the structure established by Group 1 helps us to unlock and understand just what these passages mean. For instance, Group 2 helped us understand that ancient Babylon is a foreshadowed type of the End Time's world. Ancient Babylon's city location and ancestral heritage sprung from its historical association with the Tower of Babel, where a then-unified mankind rebelled against God and His ways. The pride of ancient Babylon's king, Nebuchadnezzar, and his absolute rule, represented by the gold head of the statue in Daniel 2, points to a type of idol worship of man's achievements that will again spring up during the End Times.

These passages, particularly Daniel 2 and 7, coupled with Revelation 12–18, help us to see the progression of history towards its culmination when, finally, mankind's corrupt systems and empires will be shattered by God. Since these empires all shared in common the control of Jerusalem, conquered territory seems to be the simplest way of understanding the final empire just before God sets up His equally literal kingdom. The final array of empires will be made up of the people groups of the previous empires and of the former territory of Rome. The identity of the final kingdom points to the peoples who now live in the areas formerly occupied by the Eastern and Western Roman Empire: the nations of Europe and the Middle East.

In the case of Daniel 2, the clay not mixing with iron is a picture of two completely different systems of territorial government that do not mix but remain distinct. We can surmise that the clay parts represent a religious-oriented government, because another non-metal material, stone, represents God's kingdom. Just as man was formed from clay, these governments founded on a religion of clay will be part of a coalition with western governments

As you can see, we haven't had to force any of these to fit. Some of the passages we have looked at dealt with broader topics of the End Times and, as appropriate, I placed these broader topics (such as the succession of historical empires or the Millennium, Great White Throne Judgment, and the eternal state) in places where I've discovered that they go. Our study into the order and sequence of End Times events could easily expand into a larger study of the history of the world and God's plan to restore mankind to His intended purpose. But all that is beyond the scope of this book.

That sums up Group 2. There are no deal-breakers here. Each of these passages can be simply understood in a plain-sense way that is perfectly compatible with our current understanding of End-Times order and sequence.

18

Adding the Finishing Pieces of Group 3

Every building needs some form of finishing to be complete. There are all kinds of finishes, some special and some mundane. The finishes often tell about the taste and preferences of the designer. It is often hard for people to put their finger on just what makes one room or space feel better than another. In the design world, a space is said to have a certain *ambiance*. This means that the lighting and finishes work together to create a certain feeling and tell a certain story within the space of the building.

The rest of Scripture also tells a certain story about the End Times. We see that because God loves us, He has enacted to save us from eternal separation from Himself. We see that He must remove sin, evil, and its consequences so that we can live with Him as He intended. We see a city in the future called "New Jerusalem" where the Bride of Christ lives, works, and plays, fulfilling God's intended purposes for us. Sometimes, we get this idea that God intends for people to sit around on clouds and play harps all day, forever, but this is not so. We will simply worship God in all we do. Whether we sing, swim, or play harps, we will be doing what God intended.

As God works in the lives of men here on earth, He reminds them that the ultimate goal is reconciliation and that the events of the End Times are part of a transition towards that goal. The tertiary passages connect to the rest of Scripture and mention various aspects of the End Times in support of another topic or story being told. Their purpose is not to lay out an order and sequence of events. Rather, their purpose is to convey a message like, "It will all work out in the end." Others, like Genesis 7, only touch upon the subject of End Times in the sense that they are used as examples of how things will be.

If you take the time to read these passages, you may notice that many are not passages we would normally associate with the End Times, such as some of the psalms. While these passages all share the common characteristic of not addressing End-Times order and sequence in a clear and detailed manner (nor do they claim to), to qualify for this section, they only need to mention or allude to an End-Times event.

This is why I think of them as many "finish pieces" that provide an overall ambience of the End-Times doctrine. Individually, you don't notice them making a difference; but as a whole, many enhance our understanding of how the End Times relates to a variety of other topics in the Bible. In other words, Group 3 adds overall beauty and detail, but it doesn't hold up the structure of a building any more than Group 2.

The passages here are too numerous to address. I'll single out a few to show you how these passages can enhance our understanding. Rather than telling you why each is disqualified to be part of the first or second group, I thought it more beneficial to describe how they embellish the overall scheme we have already established. Here are some examples:

Genesis 7:1–16 describes what happened the day of the first global judgment we call "the Flood." It is a pattern that Jesus would have us see and not miss. He references it in Matt. 24:37–38 and Luke 17:26–27; and in the passage in Luke, He also ties in the days of Lot and Sodom.[57] The clear parallel in both episodes of judgment is that as soon as the righteous were secured, God's judgment began. When Noah and his family were safely in the ark, the flood waters began to fall. When Lot and his family were out of range of Sodom, fire and brimstone pulverized it. The language used in Gen. 7:12–13 could not be more explicit in telling us that on the very same day that they entered the ark, judgment fell. Those who died believed that tomorrow would come business as usual. But there's not always a tomorrow.

Psalm 2 describes events that parallel those of the seventh trumpet in Revelation when the nations realize that they have been kicked out of Jerusalem. Revelation 11:18 tells us the nations were enraged, just as they are depicted here in Psalm 2:1. No matter

---

[57] Peter also repeats the same in 2 Peter 2:5–9.

how much they plot to retake Jerusalem and Mt. Zion, they do so in vain. God laughs at their futile attempts and declares that the rebellion will be crushed. Given God's laughter in verse 4, I find it ironic that "iron" and "clay" are used here in verse 9, which aligns with how God utterly destroys the kingdoms of man at the iron and clay phase of their existence, according to Dan. 2:43–44. In fact, there are many interesting alignments with Daniel 2 and 7, including the reference to the "son" who receives the kingdoms in Dan. 2:7, 2:12. Daniel 7:13–14 shows us that it is the "son of man" who receives the kingdom; and we know that Jesus loved to refer to Himself using this title (Matt. 8:20).

Also, do you remember the unique terms that we discussed earlier, "the wrath of the lamb" (Rev. 6:16) and the "Day of Christ" (2 Thess. 2:2)? We have another one here in Psalm 2:12: "his wrath" is the "son's wrath."

Psalm 79 describes a time of extreme sadness among Judeans, not unlike how they would feel after having been betrayed by those with whom they made the final seven-year covenant. It is the final plea of a nation, broken at last and seeking God in earnest. Psalm 79 finds its End-Times alignment sometime after the temple is defiled and a full-scale assault on faithful Jews has begun, as described in Dan. 12:1.

Psalm 97 is ordered in such away that it first declares that the Lord reigns; then, fire goes before Him as He judges the earth to finally puts to shame all of the idol worshippers. I see this psalm aligning with Revelation 16 and 19, when God thoroughly judges the world and terminates its empires forever.

Psalm 118 reflects the rejoicing that the 144,000 and others will feel in the presence of the Lamb while they stand on Mt. Zion together after the seventh trumpet and before Armageddon, when the nations come to surround Jerusalem to retake it. In Psalm 118:8–9, they learn their lesson not to trust in man. In Luke 13:35, Jesus, Himself, alludes to this day of salvation for Jerusalem when He essentially quotes Psalm 118:26.

Isaiah 14:3–23 describes the fall of the king of Babylon, and yet Jesus uses Isa. 14:12 to described Satan's fall in Luke 10:18. Revelation 12:8–10 makes a similar reference. In light of our study of Babylon and the Antichrist and the dragon who empowers him (Rev. 13:2), this passage potentially takes on deeper meaning by reinforcing our understanding of the Antichrist as leader of the final "great Babylon" spanning the globe.

Daniel is a book that can contribute to our overall understanding of how God moves in history. Daniel's culture and the End-Times culture will be similar in that they both will have misplaced the Scriptures in favor of secularization. Daniel was probably a baby when the Scriptures were rediscovered in the temple during King Josiah's reign. By then, the culture of Judea had grown accustomed to living with the surrounding nations, and the brief revival spawned by Josiah was not enough to stay God's hand of judgment. Soon, the city of Jerusalem found itself surrounded by Nebuchadnezzar's armies, and its people were forced to become vassals of Babylon. Part of their tribute was to give up their young princes and wealthy youths to be trained in the wisdom of Babylon. Daniel was part of this group.

The people of Judea must have been devastated, as Babylon washed over Jerusalem like a raging sea in three successive sieges. The final siege destroyed the city and the temple, leaving only the poor to tend the land. Those who had maintained or renewed their faith during Josiah's reign a few years earlier were now challenged. How would God keep His promise to bless all nations through Abraham? What would happen to the Promised Land?

The book of Daniel is God's answer. The purpose of the book is found in Daniel's praise to God in Dan. 2:19–23; it is God who sets up and destroys kingdoms. Therefore, God is in control, and He can keep His promises. During the 70-year captivity, God spoke to Judea in a foreign tongue, as Isaiah had prophesied earlier in Isaiah 28:11. In fact, Daniel Chapters 2–7 are written in the Babylonian language called "Chaldee." They correspond approximately to the 70-year captivity and are organized in a reverse mirrored pattern, so that we can understand certain truths made by these parallels, as follows.

Chapter 2 and 7 parallel one another in describing a series of succeeding empires, beginning with Babylon and ending with an eternal kingdom that destroys an extension of the fourth kingdom. Daniel's vision in Chapter 2 came at the beginning of his captivity, so that he could comfort the mourning Judeans who had been removed from all they held familiar. His vision in Chapter 7 came towards the end of the 70-year captivity to provide hope that God was still in control.

Chapter 3 and 6 parallel each other in that they describe people of integrity who would rather die than compromise any aspect of their obedience to God. They prized a right-standing relationship with God over an extended life of compromise. What would it have hurt Daniel to close his shutters this one time before he prayed so that the others wouldn't see? None of these knew whether the fiery furnace or the lion's den would be their end. But they did know that God is in control.

Chapter 4 and 5 parallel each other by describing the fall of two arrogant and prideful kings. At the height of their hubris, God chopped them down suddenly. In Dan. 4:30, Nebuchadnezzar's statement allows us to connect his pride with that of the future "great Babylon." Chapter 5 depicts the sudden fall of Babylon the very night that king Belshazzar mocked God by having a drunken orgy with the holy utensils and cups from the temple in Jerusalem. It was that night that Cyrus, son of the east, dried up the "great Euphrates" river and snuck under the river gate like a thief to suddenly take the citadel and, consequently, Babylon. This supplies us with the basis for understanding the sixth bowl of Revelation and the events that follow it.

In total, Daniel 2–7 speaks to the complete future of the nations that dominate Israel. That is arguably why God had Daniel record this section in a Gentile language rather than Hebrew. The Gentile section speaks to the Gentile nations about their ultimate destruction and replacement by God's kingdom.

This division of the text also highlights a principle of prophecy, "near-far" fulfillment. So that we understand and recognize the ultimate fulfillment, a "near" fulfillment occurs that is close, but not exact. In the Gentile language section here, for example, we learn that there is a progression of successive empires that dominate Israel, but that will have an ultimate destructive end. Out of the fourth and last empire (or "beast," represented in the visions in chapters 2–7) arises the End-Times character we recognize as the Antichrist, who is described in Dan. 7:19–22 as a "little horn." This represents the "far" fulfillment.

The "near" fulfillment of this prophecy is recorded later, in Daniel 8, when the language of the book returns to Hebrew. Daniel 8:21–25 describes the little horn as arising out of the Greek empire, which we can identify conclusively as the third empire or beast in Daniel 2–7. The near fulfillment of this prophecy was realized in 168 B.C., when the Greek ruler Antiochus Epiphanes desecrated the Jewish temple and brutally slaughtered many Jews. Historically, Antiochus' dominion only reached part of the world, but ultimately, in the far fulfillment, the Antichrist's dominion will reach the whole world.

Chapters 9–12 continue to focus on events foreshadowed in the 160s B.C., with events that will be ultimately fulfilled in the End Times as we have already studied.

2 Thessalonians 1:4–12. As Christians suffer persecutions, they also fellowship with Christ, for He suffered greatly. This is why Christians are worthy to inherit the Kingdom of God headed by the Lord Jesus Christ. Suffering is expected as part of the Christian experience during the time before Christ's return. This correlates with Revelation's perseverance of the saints.

Using the Key

Many more passages could be cited, but the main point is that the key to unlocking these passages is first unlocking what the clearest and most detailed passages have to say on the subject. Otherwise, we would be guessing or just hitting upon general meanings. In the same way that we don't change a building's foundation just because we don't want to cut off the end of a piece of finishing trim that is too long, we do not change an End-Times order and sequence just to suit a pet interpretation of a secondary (or tertiary) passage. Our task is not building a doctrine of our own imagination, but one that can be developed by working around our own biases.

You can plainly see how a person could take many of these verses and develop all kinds of various End Times doctrines. Without a way to interpret the passages that is as consistent and simple as connecting dots, we could easily end up with declaring views such as the "last trump" or a "secret Rapture" disconnected from the Second Coming, or even declaring that all this occurred symbolically sometime in the past.

As you continue to study, I'm sure that you will see that the truth of this method will continue to bear itself out as being valid and useful in seeing the wonderful coherency of God's Word.

Passages that deal with standing firm in the face of persecution and even death will take on new meaning if you had once been a pre-tribber. A new appreciation for God's love may overwhelm you if you were formerly a post-tribber, when you understand what all the shortened times refer to and why we need to be purified to avoid being objects of God's wrath. Preterists and amillennialists may find that Bible prophecy can easily be literally true in our near future rather than requiring spiritualization or allegorization by those whose perspectives are molded by their own times.

19

Architectural Appreciation 101

> As our tour group approached the next structure near some outdoor living quarters of the monastery, our guide stopped to show us a house-sized, man-made rock outcropping with a beautiful fountain spilling down its side.
>
> "Does anybody know the purpose of the waterfall?" he asked.
>
> The group proposed some answers:
>
> "For serenity."
>
> "For meditation."
>
> "To reflect on one's life."
>
> Our guide smiled broadly and responded, "No, it's for the ladies restroom."

The simple answer is often overlooked. In this example, we came up with a variety of deep meanings for the waterfall, but in reality, it was simply a decorative item for the entry to the women's lavatory. Often, we approach prophecy the same way, tending to make up meaning rather than looking for the obvious similarities and connections that are already there. We like to take things further or invent grand schemes when there is really nothing more to it than simply connecting the dots. The answer to understanding the sequence and order of the End Times is really this simple. It's quite humbling to our human pride and intellect to realize that *we* are the problem.

Who would have thought, given all the symbolic language of prophecy, that we would only need to find the clearest and most detailed passages on the topic of End-Times sequences and then compare them to each other, looking for commonalities? It *is* really that simple! It takes the emphasis off human bias and puts it back on the coherency of God's Word. There are only so many passages in the Bible on the topic of End-Times sequences. Of those, there are only a handful that are detailed, specific, and clear. These represent God's clearest counsel on the matter. It is obvious that they should agree. It is even more humbling that they *do* agree and logically develop a timeline, a structure for a doctrine.

The core structure as laid out in Chapter 16 of this book remains valid and is the basis for understanding all the other End-Times scriptures. If the doctrine of the End Times were an actual building, its detail would be incomprehensible. We could easily spend the rest of our lives appreciating its fine craftsmanship. New patterns, both large and small scale, would reveal themselves, depending on our level of examination. Even though the shape is clear, I hope to continue to study and appreciate its overwhelming beauty, a tribute to its Creator.

God is the Chief Architect of prophecy. He has ordained these clear and specific passages, and we have discovered their coherency through alignments, parallels, and various connections. It would be ludicrous to ignore many of these connections in favor of a pet theology that places events to fit into a pre-determined view. The picture has always been in God's Word. It's just been obscured by man's bias and presupposition.

> Call to Me and I will answer you, and I will tell you great and mighty things, which you do not know. (Jer. 33:3)

Appendix A

A Practical Example

Originally, I began my study in the fashion shown on the next page. I found it beneficial to reorganize the text into line numbers to read the message with new eyes. If I had included these in the book, the size would have burgeoned to something quite unmanageable. Perhaps someday there will be a way to release a detailed study to those who are interested. But if you are really *that* interested, I encourage you first to do the study in this or a similar format for yourself so that the Spirit can speak to you directly. Use the opposite chart as a guide to developing your own study of these passages.

Daniel 9:24-27	L	V	Comments with line numbers referenced
Seventy weeks are determined upon thy people and upon thy holy city, to finish the transgression, and to make an end of sins, and to make reconciliation for iniquity, and to bring in everlasting righteousness, and to seal up the vision and prophecy, and to anoint the most Holy. Know therefore and understand, that from the going forth of the commandment to restore and to build Jerusalem unto the Messiah the Prince shall be seven weeks, and threescore and two weeks: the street shall be built again, and the wall, even in troublous times. And after threescore and two weeks shall Messiah be cut off, but not for himself: and the people of the prince that shall come shall destroy the city and the sanctuary; and the end thereof shall be with a flood, and unto the end of the war desolations are determined. And he shall confirm the covenant with many for one week: and in the midst of the week he shall cause the sacrifice and the oblation to cease, and for the overspreading of abominations he shall make it desolate, even until the consummation, and that determined shall be poured upon the desolate.	1 5 10 15 20 25 30 35 37	24 25 26 27	(1-3) *70 sevens are decreed for Israel and Jerusalem:* (3-4) To finish national moral/religious rebellion. (4-5) To end habitual sinfulness and its penalty. (5-6) To atone and pardon for moral evil/wickedness. (7-8) To bring in *eternal/permanent* righteousness and justice. (8-9) To make an end of revelation and prophecy. (10) To anoint the Holy of Holies, possibly as King of kings in context with line 14, 21-2's reference to the Messiah. (10-14) From the day of the command to rebuild Jerusalem (which occurred around 446 BC—see Nehemiah 2:4-8) there shall be 7x7s (49 years) until the city is rebuilt with plaza and moats (13-14, 17-18), plus 62x7s (434 years) until Jesus is crucified (14-15, 19-21). If we take (7+62) x 7 = 483 years of 360 prophetic "pre-Flood" days (Gen. 7:11, 24, 8:3, 4) that need to be converted into current "post-Flood" solar days (365.24) days = 476 yrs, 445BC – 476 yrs = 31 AD+ (see footnote 4) = Jesus' last week leading up to His sacrificial death by crucifixion. (21) "but not for himself" = will have nothing. This implies that the Messiah will have no kingdom at this time because the people of the prince (Romans, 22) will come and destroy Jerusalem and the Temple (23-4) with the end process being an overflowing (25), and until the end, there will be war with the inevitable consequences (26-7). (27-28) He = "of the people of the prince" = the beast/antichrist = leader of the "Beast" Empire, shall confirm a (new or existing) seven-year (70th Seven) treaty (28-9). At the midpoint (29), the Beast will stop duty to God (30-31) and make an abomination of desolation (33-34) on a wing/corner (32) of the altar (where the offerings and sacrifices have been stopped) until the desolator's own end happens as determined (34-7). The idea of "pouring" out God's wrath upon this person is mentioned here at the end.

* How do we know that this command is the correct one as opposed to other ones in 2 Chron. 36:22–23, Ezra 1:1–4, 6:1–5 (note what Isa. 44:28 and 45:13 say), and in Ezra 6:6–12, 7:11–26? The answer is simple: none of these literally fit the qualifier of the wall being rebuilt in troublous times (lines 19–21). Only the Nehemiah command fits this literally (read Nehemiah 4). Additionally, Nehemiah 2 literally refers to rebuilding the city and gives us a more precise date in history to work from.

Appendix B

Is There a Gap Between the 69th and 70th Sevens?

Daniel breaks up the 70 sets of seven into three divisions: 7, 42, and 1. The last one is called the 70th Seven and it is the one that is broken up into two halves by an Abomination of Desolation. Let's look at six reasons that a gap between the 69th and 70th Seven is the natural understanding of this passage:

1. Two types of covenants

One aspect in understanding the intended meaning of the gap between the 69th and 70th sevens is to understand the difference between the two types of covenants shown to us in the Bible. One type is conditional and the other type is unconditional. The conditional covenant is commonly referred to as the "Mosaic Covenant." This covenant was given to Moses for Israel in Deuteronomy 27–28. If Israel's people obeyed, they were blessed; if they disobeyed, they were cursed. The Babylonian captivity in which Daniel was a part (Daniel 9) is the result of Israel's failure to uphold her end of the conditional Mosaic Covenant.

The unconditional covenant is commonly called the "Abrahamic Covenant." God gave this covenant to Abraham in Genesis chapters 12–17. God made this covenant with Abraham regardless of what Abraham or his descendants did. He even put Abraham to sleep during the "signing" of the covenant so that Abraham could not foolishly agree to something he could never uphold. The Abrahamic Covenant is a binding agreement from God that promises physical land, a nation, and a blessing to Abraham's offspring. God will make good on His pledge, regardless of Israel's waywardness. It is the Abrahamic Covenant that brought hardened Israel out of Egypt for the sake of the next generation to inherit the Promised Land. The future Millennium is seen by many to be the fulfillment of that covenant, whereby God will make good on all six of His promises given in Dan. 9:24. If 490-year period of 70 sets of seven had continued unbroken, this period would have expired in the first century and the covenant would not have been fulfilled. Rather, the opposite occurred. Rome came and destroyed the city and sanctuary scattering the Jews to the four winds.

This leads us to the next reason, the literal fulfillment.

2. Literal fulfillment

After the first seven sets of seven, the city and walls of Jerusalem were rebuilt as predicted. This was meant to be a sure sign for what was to follow some 62 sets far in the future—the long awaited Messiah would be cut off from the land of the living. Sure enough, after 69 sets of seven, or 483 prophetic years, the Messiah was cut off and executed on a Roman cross.

Once, even twice, God literally fulfills the prophecies given to Daniel. Therefore, He will fulfill the third one, too, by literally bringing to pass the six events of Dan. 9:24. None of those six events have yet been fulfilled in the same plain sense as the fulfillments after the seventh and 62 sets of seven.

What *did* happen after the Messiah was cut off? This leads us to the next reason, the historical record.

3. Historical record

If we take this timeline literally and at face value for which it has proven itself worthy, we end up at 32 A.D. for the end of the 69th set of seven when the Messiah was cut off.[58] If the 70th Seven

---

[58] If you use the decree of 444/445 BC recorded in Nehemiah 2, you end up with a date of 32 A.D. Nehemiah's account in Chapter 4 best fits Dan. 9:26's qualifier that the 70 Sevens would begin when the city is rebuilt in troublous times. However, there were some earlier decrees, beginning with Cyrus the first year of his reign after he overthrew Babylon in 539/8 B.C., that some point to as a valid start date for the 70 Sevens, as well, particularly in light of Jer. 25:11 and Isa. 44:28. If this earlier date is used, you arrive at the date 63 B.C. rather than 31 A.D. This earlier date is significant because it is the year Rome took control of Jerusalem.

is continuous, we should be able to identify a seven-year covenant that was made immediately afterwards, followed by an abomination of the temple in Jerusalem three and one-half years later, just as Daniel 9 lays out.

But where is that event? Nothing happened to the temple in 35 A.D. The six promises of Daniel 9:24 were not literally fulfilled at that time. Therefore, the literal fulfillment of these events must be awaiting some other time. Hence, a gap. Why? Because the nation had rejected their Anointed One, Yeshua (Jesus). Only He could literally fulfill all six events by literally reigning from Zion. Jesus publicly explained to Israel what was to happen in Luke 21 while He taught in the temple.

This leads us to the purpose of a gap: the Time of the Gentiles.

4. The Time of the Gentiles

Israel had not been about their purpose of evangelizing the world and spreading the blessing of Abraham abroad. God promised Abraham that all nations would be blessed through his seed (Genesis). To see that this would happen, God sent the gospel out to the world. As other writers addressed (Paul in Romans 11 and John in Revelation 11 and 14), we see that the completion of this time is at the end of the 70th Seven when all Israel will not only be saved, but receive the fulfilled promises.

5. Biblical context

Is there a biblical precedent for this? Does God use gaps elsewhere? Are there other prophecies in the Bible that describe a "gap" between the First Coming and the Second Coming? Yes, we can look at Isa. 9:6–7, Isa. 61:1–2, and Zech. 9:9–10:

> For unto us a child is born, unto us a son is given: and the government shall be upon his shoulder: and his name shall be called Wonderful, Counsellor, the mighty God, the everlasting Father, the Prince of Peace. >>GAP<< Of the increase of his government and peace there shall be no end, upon the throne of David, and upon his kingdom, to order it,

---

Rather than arguing for either/or, there may be room to see both dates covering different aspects of the End Times.

147

and to establish it with judgment and with justice from henceforth even for ever. The zeal of the LORD of hosts will perform this. (Isaiah 9:6–7)

The Spirit of the Lord GOD is upon me; because the LORD hath anointed me to preach good tidings unto the meek; he hath sent me to bind up the brokenhearted, to proclaim liberty to the captives, and the opening of the prison to them that are bound; >>GAP<< To proclaim the acceptable year of the LORD, and the day of vengeance of our God; to comfort all that mourn. (Isaiah 61:1–2)

Rejoice greatly, O daughter of Zion; shout, O daughter of Jerusalem: behold, thy King cometh unto thee: he is just, and having salvation; lowly, and riding upon an ass, and upon a colt the foal of an ass. >>GAP<< And I will cut off the chariot from Ephraim, and the horse from Jerusalem, and the battle bow shall be cut off: and he shall speak peace unto the heathen: and his dominion shall be from sea even to sea, and from the river even to the ends of the earth. (Zech 9:9–10)

6. Events after the 69 sevens

Daniel 9:26 describes three significant events that must occur after 69 of the sevens are complete. The text is very specific about this. Keep in mind that these three things relate specifically to Daniel's people, the Jews; and Jerusalem, the holy city. These three things are:

1) The Messiah will be cut off, dying to save others.
2) The people (nation) of the "prince" will come and destroy the city and the temple.
3) Unto the end, the area will be war-torn.

The first item could happen in very little time; however, the second could take years to accomplish; and the third (if "the end" is taken literally) refers to the Time of the Gentiles and will take millennia to fulfill. Indeed, it takes no stretch of the imagination to see how the sacrificial death of the Messiah, the subsequent destruction of Jerusalem (initially in 70 A.D. and, ultimately, the nation in 132 A.D.), and even how Jerusalem has been fought over from the Crusades to the founding of the nation today, warrants — even *demands* — a gap between the 69th and 70th sevens.

Given these points, it is quite sound and logical to see a gap and its purpose: to accomplish in the world what Israel would not do, allowing Israel to see that they can not trust in man; then, finally restore them into a right relationship with God so that they can fully receive the promises given to Abraham.

Appendix C

Luke 21: Private or Public?

When I first tried to understand the meaning of the Olivet Discourse, I started with three passages: Matthew 24–25, Mark 13, and Luke 21. I started a study sheet with three columns and placed them in order and began circling the common phrases and alignments. I soon found that Luke 21 did not align. In fact, if I forced it to align, I ended up with a timing contradiction of "before" in Luke 21:12 with "then" in Matt. 24:9. At that point, I began to look for the differences rather than the similarities and discovered many more of them.

A detailed understanding of the differences between Matthew 24, Mark 13, and Luke 21 cannot be overstated. Despite certain similarities at the beginnings and the ends, they are not recording the same account. There is a clear gap between the time and place the disciples asked about the buildings and where and when Jesus explained their relationship to the end of the age. In Matt. 24:3, Matthew even goes out of his way to tell us that this is a private discussion. Mark adds that in addition to it being a being private discussion, only Peter, James, John, and Andrew were present (Mark 13:3). This is in stark contrast to the context of Luke, in which the discussion never leaves the temple venue.

Luke explains his differing account at the end of Chapter 21 in verses 37–38, when he tells us:

> And in the day time he was teaching in the temple; and at night he went out, and abode in the mount that is called the mount of Olives. And all the people came early in the morning to him in the temple, for to hear him. (Luke 21:37–38)

Therefore, it is reasonable to see the Luke 21 passage being taught in the temple publicly during the day, while Matthew 24 and Mark 13 record the private explanation given to the disciples later that evening on the Mount of Olives. This would also explain the differences between the questions the disciples asked. The questions in Luke 21, while Jesus taught in the temple, were specifically about when the temple was to be destroyed:

> And they asked him, saying, Master, but when shall these things be? and what sign will there be when these things shall come to pass? (Luke 21:7)

By contrast, the questions in Matthew 24 and Mark 13 dealt with issues brought up in the Luke 21 account:

> Tell us, when shall these things be? and what shall be the sign of thy coming, and of the end of the world? (Matt. 24:3)

When Jesus answered these questions, He tied this event indirectly to the time of the end and His return. It is a common pattern in the gospels for Jesus to explain to the disciples privately what He taught publicly.

> And he said unto them, Unto you it is given to know the mystery of the kingdom of God: but unto them that are without, all these things are done in parables. (Mark 4:11)

This explains the difference in the questions first asked publicly in Luke 21 and then the more refined questions asked in Matthew 24 and Mark 13.

All three passages begin similarly, with a discussion of events that loosely parallel the seal events of Revelation. However, Luke makes a 180-degree turn from Matthew 24 beginning in verse 12: "But before all these..." Matthew, on the other hand, continues along the same stream of thought and discusses the events that happen next: "Then shall they..." (Matt. 24:9). The timing of the differing accounts do not rejoin again until the mention of Jesus' return.

The differences in the interim sections are many. It is clear that while Jesus has the public ear in the temple, as recorded in

Luke 21, He explains the then-future destruction of Jerusalem and the temple in 70 A.D. He elaborates on this theme by telling the people and teachers of Israel that Jerusalem will be trodden down until the Time of the Gentiles is fulfilled (Luke 21:24). There is no mention of the Time of the Gentiles in the Olivet Discourse passages of Matthew 24 and Mark 13. Even the type of abominations and distress are different in severity.

When one ponders how these accounts were written and who wrote them, it explains why they are different. One of Jesus' disciples wrote the book of Matthew. He was privy to the inner circle of Jesus' clear and direct teaching. Mark was Peter's interpreter. He recorded the teachings of Peter, a disciple of Jesus. Luke was a Gentile convert who traveled to Judea to interview eyewitnesses to develop his account. It is likely he found the time to interview many people who were in the temple that day.

In other words, Matthew and Mark recorded the private conversation between Jesus and His disciples, while Luke's account focused on the public sermon:

> Forasmuch as many have taken in hand to set forth in order a declaration of those things which are most surely believed among us, Even as they delivered them unto us, which from the beginning were eyewitnesses, and ministers of the word; It seemed good to me also, having had perfect understanding of all things from the very first, to write unto thee in order, most excellent Theophilus, That thou mightest know the certainty of those things, wherein thou hast been instructed. (Luke 1:1–4)

Therefore, when you read these various passages, recognize that they are directed at different audiences for different purposes. Luke 21's Temple Discourse is directed to a broader audience that included more than just Jesus' disciples. Its purpose was to answer what would happen to the temple in the future and what people should do at that time. When Jesus spoke of the temple being destroyed (Luke 21:6), He knew that there were to be two future destructions of the temple (in 70 A.D. and at a time yet future). He answered both together for the sake of "all who had an ear" to hear in Israel. He started with the three signs that we know of as corresponding to seals that lead up to the ultimate defilement of the temple in the End Times to signify its predominance. But "before these things," and to show a distinct difference, Jesus lays out the more present trials that His followers will have to endure before the siege of Jerusalem only 38 years in the future. It is then, before the siege tightens its knot to desolate Jerusalem (Luke 21:20–21), that they must flee into the wilderness. Historically, Christians in Jerusalem did just that. As they saw the approaching Roman legions under Titus, they managed to escape before it was too late. Jerusalem was indeed trampled then and again in 132 A.D., becoming farmland for Rome. Since then, the nations have controlled and still lay hold of many parts of Jerusalem, defiling even the Temple Mount with temples to one of their "gods."

Jesus knew all this, especially that the Time of the Gentiles would extend up to the very last defilement when He returns. Thus, to answer one question, He had to answer both. The destruction of the first leads to the destruction of the latter. In the second group of scriptures, we see that the fourth kingdom, Rome and its offspring, extends to the establishment of God's literal and eternal kingdom. No other empire ever replaced Rome as much as it fragmented into other versions of itself.

When we look to the purpose of the Olivet Discourse recorded in Matthew 24 and Mark 13, we see that it is directed specifically to Jesus' disciples, who are known today as Christians. The "you" of the Olivet Discourse did not have a broader audience. In fact, our comparison of these passages confirms that "you" is not directed to Israel in general (meaning those who may or may not believe in Christ); rather, it is directed to those who have an ear to believe. When Jesus refers to "you" in Matthew 24 and Mark 13, know that He is talking only to Peter, James, John, and Andrew.

The common event in all three passages appears to be a discussion involving the wonderfully designed temple building. Jesus responds by saying that these buildings will be destroyed eventually. In Matthew 24 and Mark 13, the account stops there, until, in verse 3, Jesus' disciples reappear on the Mount of Olives that evening and approach Him privately, for they had heard what He said about the trial coming against the whole world.

Jesus' words from the temple, as recorded in Luke 21:35–36, must have still been ringing in their ears:

> For as a snare shall it come on all them that dwell on the face of the whole earth. Watch ye therefore, and pray always, that ye may be accounted worthy to escape all these things that shall come to pass, and to stand before the Son of man. (Luke 21:35–36)

They also knew these events involved Jesus' return.

> And then shall they see the Son of man coming in a cloud with power and great glory. (Luke 21:27)

These things allowed them to reformulate their questions to better understand what He had earlier spoken publicly in the hearing of all Israel.

> Tell us, when shall these things be? and what shall be the sign of thy coming, and of the end of the world? (Matt. 24:3)

These passages are similar, but not the same. They align, but only in the sense that the Olivet Discourse is a private explanation of the earlier Temple Discourse and elaborates on subjects in response to the revised questions focusing on Christ's return.

About the Author

Cameron Fultz lives in Ellensburg, Washington, where he is a licensed architect. He is also an elder with his local fellowship and is a teacher of the Bible. His passion is to equip believers with the tools they need to understand God's Word for themselves.

Cameron has been married to his wife, Teresa, for 15 years and has five great children: Erica, Katrina, Andrea, Noah, and Olivia.

QUICK ORDER FORM

Prophecy's Architecture
by Cameron Fultz

A detailed look at how one determines an end-times doctrine. Written from the perspective of a professional architect, it uses the examples of architecture to illustrate the basics of biblical exposition, gradually building an end-times doctrine block by block to determine its timing and sequence.

157 pages. $14.95.

 # Copies _____
Total Merchandise: $ _____
USPS Priority Mail shipping included

Please send check or money order to:

Strong Tower Publishing
P.O. Box 973
Milesburg, PA 16853

For credit card orders:

Strong Tower Publishing will accept credit card orders through PayPal. Send payment to: strongtowerpubs@aol.com.

Pricing good through 2005.
For updated shipping and pricing information, visit our Web site at www.strongtowerpublishing.com.

Printed in the United States
73997LV00002B/47

9 780970 433060